GOD HAS FEELINGS TOO

Heather.
from. Sue. A.
20/1/87.

God Has Feelings Too

ALEX BUCHANAN

KINGSWAY PUBLICATIONS
EASTBOURNE

ISBN 0 86065 351 X

Unless otherwise indicated biblical quotations are from the
New American Standard Bible © The Lockman Foundation
1960, 1962, 1963, 1968, 1971, 1972, 1973

Front cover photo: Photo Library International

Printed in Great Britain for
KINGSWAY PUBLICATIONS LTD
Lottbridge Drove, Eastbourne, E. Sussex BN23 6NT by
Cox & Wyman Ltd, Reading.
Typeset by Nuprint Services Ltd, Harpenden, Herts.

Contents

To
Peggy
my darling wife
and my best
friend

Preface

I have been prodded into writing this book. My previous reluctance was due to the knowledge that I am neither a scholar nor a theologian. I tend to speak out of the heart more than the head, which often makes for untidy writing. I am putting pen to paper now, simply to share whatever thoughts and insights I may have with a new generation of 'apprentice kings and queens'. I hope that I will inspire them with a deep love for the Lord Jesus: to know him as a real person; to share his own emotions and to press on with his warfare in the light of them.

I want to testify to God's great grace and courage in his dealings with me and to praise him for what I can only describe as his loving ruthlessness in them. He has chastened me with a thousand scourgings and lifted me up after a thousand falls. He has broken my heart with many reproofs but healed it with many healings. This book has come out of much experience both on the mountain tops and in the valleys. The latter have been my best school and I have learned more in them than on the high peaks. In nearly forty years of sickness, pain and frequent surgery, God has been working away at the task of making an ordinary man into a king—a wreck into a servant of God. May this encourage others who feel as weak as I do to press on with God.

In writing this book, I am indebted to my beloved wife for her constant encouragement and support. In her life, as well as mine, God has been at work, producing a faith and perseverance that have triumphed in the face of many years of sickness. I am also greatly indebted to many of my friends and spiritual mentors whose knowledge and teaching have so enriched my life. Their wisdom has been stored up in my heart for many years, passed on to some extent in my pastoral and itinerant ministry, and hopefully now expressed in this volume.

'I do love you, Lord, may these pages somehow show it.'

ALEX BUCHANAN

I

The Feelings of God

It was many years after I became a Christian before I realized that God has feelings. My concept of God was coloured by scriptures such as John 4:24, 'God is spirit.' Who can understand or explain a spirit? Can a spirit really have feelings? Again, 1 Timothy 6:16 speaks of a God who 'dwells in light unapproachable, whom no man can see'. For me God was a real and glorious Deity indeed, and certainly my Saviour, but hardly close and communicative. He ruled the universe and had everything worked out and under control: a God quite unruffled by human activities. Impartial, impassive, perfect and self-sufficient, but not a God who would embrace me when I was frightened or readily forgive me when I had sinned.

So I grew up watching my Ps and Qs as far as God was concerned, longing to love him but too afraid to get near enough to do so. I carried out a sort of 'evangelical penance' at intervals so that God would not be too hard on me, but at the same time I was tormented by the fear that it would not be enough. I longed to get to heaven but rather dreaded to be for ever with One who was thrice holy and knew me through and through. There was an ache in my heart which grew more and more intense. I longed to know God but didn't know how. But

9

God met me in my need. Through his Holy Spirit he gave
me a vision of Jesus and I fell deeply in love with him. It
was after this experience that the Scriptures came alive
for me, revealing the feelings of God.

John says, 'The Word became flesh, and dwelt among
us, and we beheld His glory, glory as of the only begotten
from the Father, full of grace and truth' (Jn 1:14). Jesus
said, 'He who has seen Me has seen the Father' (Jn
14:9). God came in a form with which we could identify.
How merciful! If God had appeared in all his glory as
Creator, none could have lived before him, for our
minds are too small even to conceive it, let alone see it.
Our inherent sin would also have made it impossible to
stand before him.

All this is not to imply that Jesus did not manifest the
glory of God but to emphasize the loving understanding
of the Godhead in that the Father revealed himself to us
in the form of a man. Jesus was God in the flesh, with
hands, feet, eyes and ears. A person who could be seen
and approached, even touched. His facial expression
could be seen to alter as he saw those who were sick,
lonely and oppressed by the devil. If he had remained in
'unapproachable light' (1 Tim 6:16), no one could have
reached him, but he was 'found in appearance as a man'
(Phil 2:8) so that men could come to him with safety. Far
from being an impassive God, he came and lived among
us as a real person pulsating with life and love. An
outreaching God with arms spread wide even to the
sinful and unlovely, even to a leper and a Judas. A God
who does indeed feel grief, anger, joy and compassion.
Who 'loves righteousness and hates iniquity'. I no longer
believe in an unfeeling and remote God, so clinically
holy that he refuses even to look at the sinful. Habakkuk
1:13 says that God cannot remain unmoved when he
looks on sin, not that he cannot look on it at all.

Having said this I want to make it crystal clear that I do

believe in a thrice holy God; a supreme Creator; One before whom we must bow in reverence and complete submission. But I also believe in a tender-hearted God who feels with us and for us in our weaknesses. Yes, God has feelings too, but they are not characterized by the mercurial ups and downs common to human feelings. He is not a sad God whom we must cheer up, nor a needy God for whom we must provide. He is not an angry Deity whom we must appease lest he lose control of his emotions. His anger does not blow hot and cold, nor does his love wax and wane, nor does it degenerate into mere sentimentality. His anger is pure anger, his love is pure love. The instability of our emotions causes us to be weak and vulnerable. God's feelings, however, are pure and completely balanced, 'For I, the Lord, do not change' (Mal 3:6).

Many dangers beset those who seek to portray God, not least that of imbalance. Any attempt to describe his humanity brings a risk of neglecting his deity, and vice versa. I feel that today we hear more about the greatness of God than his goodness. In the church there are teachers who are experts in exegesis and masters of theology. Erudite and eloquent they delineate the greatness of God, but time and again it is a God who is far removed from man. A God of rules and regulations; a demanding Deity who does not suffer fools gladly. Such teachers depress me. Their preaching may be full of material prowess, but it turns my blood to water, and robs me of hope by painting a caricature of the real God.

Conversely there are others who emphasize the humanity of God to the extent that he becomes a mere buddy, a good old God who turns up trumps when we whine loudly enough. A God who is quite dazzled by our candy floss worship and crooning love songs. A sweet and sentimental Jesus who is really far too nice to punish or destroy. I could not worship a God who is only a larger version of myself; who can be wheedled and wangled into my way of doing things. Neither could I worship an ice-cold Maker who would disdain my costliest offering because it fell short of his perfect standard.

Scripture shows us a God who longs to be known. He sent prophet after prophet to tell men about himself. In Hebrews 1:1 we read that 'God...spoke long ago to the fathers in the prophets in many portions and in many ways'. He spoke to them from mountains, out of burning bushes and clouds, and through miracle after miracle—until finally he sent his Son who was the Word made flesh, God's message to men. I can imagine myriads of enthralled angels watching God set the scene for the birth of Jesus, perhaps scarcely able to comprehend what God was doing. He was going to bare his heart to the sons of men. He was going to take sinful wretches and change them. He was going to invite them to sit on thrones and know the secrets of eternity. No stand-offish God here, but One who was and is ready to share himself with men, to give them all but his deity. 'He who did not spare his own Son, but delivered Him up for us all, how will He not also with Him freely give us all things?' (Rom 8:32). All through the ages God's cry has been 'come unto me', and this is still his cry today. How tragic when he also has to say to some, 'You would not come to me that you may have life.'

God has made it possible for us to draw near to him through Jesus, the 'new and living way' (Heb 1:20), and has invited us to come boldly to the throne of grace. And as if that is not enough he enables us through Scripture to know what he is like. In it he uses human terms to describe himself, and this helps me to relate to him too.

Meditating on the Scriptures is one of the greatest ways of knowing God, especially dwelling on the many glorious cameos of Christ which make him so real and near. It is through these that he is revealed, his eyes shining with love, yet steely when they see our sin. His hands offering us 'all things to enjoy' (1 Tim 6:17), yet chastening us often, urging us onward, holding us back; strengthening our hands to wield the sword of the Lord; caressing our brow when we feel weary and faint. What a God! For me one of the loveliest portrayals of the Lord Jesus is found in the Song of Solomon 5:10–16. The beloved stands with glowing face, and with tremendous ardour speaks intimately of the one whom she knows and loves. She dwells upon the beauty of her lover who is both divine and human, radiant and ruddy. She describes in passionate terms his head, eyes, cheeks, lips, hands and feet, concluding with the glorious words, 'This is my beloved and this is my friend.'

An increasing knowledge of God as opposed to knowledge about God brings an increasing love into the hearts of those who earnestly seek after him. Such love and knowledge will revolutionize our prayer life, creating a deep relationship with a real person.

As we meditate upon the feelings of God in the following chapters, may we constantly keep uppermost in our minds the essential truth that God has revealed himself to us so that we might know him and love him and so find abundant, everlasting life.

STOP AND THINK

Do you *really* believe that the almighty, everlasting God, ruler of the universe, all-knowing and all-powerful, has feelings?

2

A God of Compassion

I love the word compassion. It has several shades of meaning, all of which reflect something of its beauty. Compassion means sympathy, suffering with or on behalf of others and being afflicted with their affliction. It means mercy, refraining from anger or judgement, even though it may be totally justified. It means understanding, seeing clearly into a person's situation and sharing it with them. Again, it means longsuffering, patiently bearing with others despite their weaknesses.

Our God is a God of great compassion and Scripture abounds with evidence of this. Consider his tender-hearted compassion described in Psalm 23, 'He makes me lie down in green pastures; He leads me beside quiet waters.' He guides, restores and feeds us even when enemies are around. The Lord's compassion for us is like the ever attentive care of the shepherd for his weary, wandering sheep. 'Like a shepherd He will tend His flock, in His arm He will gather the lambs, and carry them in His bosom; He will gently lead the nursing ewes' (Is 40:11). The 'great Shepherd of the sheep' (Heb 13:20), the Lord Jesus himself 'seeing the multitudes ...felt compassion for them, because they were distressed and downcast like sheep without a shepherd' (Mt 9:36). This compassion extended to the individual within the crowd. The Lord went out of his way to meet the needs of those rejected by men. He had pity for the blind men and reached out to them (Mt 20:34), and also to the leper (Mk 1:41). I heard a beautiful story of a woman who many years ago visited a home for diseased prostitutes. Their bodies were so ravaged that a fan was kept going to divert the stench from the visitors who of course stayed well away from them. This woman was so full of God's compassion that she went and embraced them all, stroking their faces and praying with them. Like Jesus, she reached out to those who were considered the dregs of society.

Psalm 72:13 speaks of a God who has compassion on the poor and needy: he will save and rescue them. Whether our poverty is spiritual, circumstantial or emotional, a compassionate God stands by to rescue us. If even a sparrow falling to the ground does not escape the notice of God, how can a poor human being go unnoticed?

The Lord's compassion is gracious and forgiving, sensitive to the situation of the individual. The angel at the empty tomb told the women to 'go, tell His disciples and Peter...' (Mk 16:7). Amidst the triumph and joy of the resurrection, the Lord took particular care to assure Peter of his complete forgiveness for his denial.

Psalm 78:38 tells us that a compassionate God did not wipe out those who merited destruction, but restrained his anger and forgave them. We are among them, both as individuals and a nation. Britain has become a pagan land. A few years ago I gave a prophecy in which God said: 'Because my church has become apathetic and has failed to guard the walls of the nation, because the land has rejected my laws and become steeped in iniquity, you shall become a prey to every foul spirit.' Yet even in that judgemental word there was hope and compassion because the prophecy went on: 'But when I hear the renewed cry of the intercessors and see my people manifesting righteousness, I will yet deliver the nation from final judgement by restraining my wrath.'

God's compassion is fatherly

In the words of Psalm 103:13–14 we can hear the very heartbeat of God. Compassion pours out of that great heart. Sympathy, mercy, understanding and long-suffering are all lavished on those who fear him. Not only does he know our frame but he remembers that we are only dust. He knows all about us because he is God and nothing whatever can be hidden from him. I am not at all surprised that he knows, but I am constantly thrilled by the fact that he remembers me. With the whole of creation to enjoy and all of heaven to absorb him; with myriads of glorious angels to gladden his heart by their unceasing worship and complete obedience, he might well overlook the frailty of one of the 4,500 million people on earth, but he does not! He cares, he understands, he makes allowances for our humanity. What tremendous encouragement and hope we can gather from considering the compassion of God. Let us draw near and bask in his mercy and grace, his sympathy and care. When we do so we will be heartened to press on with his great work. How approachable and understanding is our God, and how different from the God portrayed by some as only too ready and able to spot the minutest weakness and the smallest failure, and very efficient in punishing both.

God's compassion is wonderfully tender. 'A bruised reed He will not break, and a dimly burning wick he will not extinguish' (Is 42:3). If God sees a man battered, dispirited and defeated he does not brush him aside. He takes this bruised reed and heals him. In ancient times the reed gatherers were looking only for reeds which would make good quill pens or good writing paper. They would reject any broken reed as useless; their time was too valuable to spend on sub-standard material. But God is different. He specializes in making kings out of convicts, rulers out of rebels.

When an eastern householder saw the wick of his lamp smouldering and the light growing dim, he would often throw the whole lamp out as rubbish, but when God sees one of his people flickering, their spirits low, he offers fresh oil, cleansing and renewal. My work these days is very much with leaders, many of whom are tired, dispirited and crushed. Many feel that they have failed God by losing their early zeal, and they therefore live in constant fear that he may disqualify them. How wonderful to be able to point these dear men and women to the God of infinite compassion and to say to them, 'Our God said, "Heaven and earth will pass away, but my words will not pass away..." (Mk 13:31), and these words plainly say, "His compassions never fail" (Lam 3:22). Believe this, jump into his arms and enjoy his compassion.'

Isaiah gives us another lovely picture of God's compassion in Isaiah 61:1–3. God comes to a rebellious, sinful, unworthy people and brings them good news. He offers them healing, comfort, liberation and joy in exchange for mourning. Why does he bother? Why not give them over to their sin? The answer lies in our subject. He is a God of immense compassion, willing to pour it out upon them the instant they call upon him for his mercy.

Pause a moment and consider your own situation. Do you need anything from the God of Isaiah 61? Are you disheartened, crushed, worn out, overwhelmed by a sense of failure? Reach out to a compassionate God and let him enfold you. God will pour out his fatherly compassion upon you if you draw near to him.

In considering God's compassion, we should always remember that he does not condone rebellion. He will abundantly pardon, but only when confession is made and humility shown. His compassion does not make him sentimental. Even the prodigal father (why will we talk about the prodigal son?) waited until the son humbled himself, but the moment the son did so, his father ran to hug him out of heartfelt love and compassion. Because God says that he does not change and because he is not a liar, we can be sure that he is still reaching out to men today. Scripture is not just a history book, it is a reminder to every generation that God cares for and feels for man. He has an immense capacity for mercy which no one can ever exhaust. 'For high as the heavens are above the earth, so great is His lovingkindness towards those who fear him' (Ps 103:11).

Years ago a young man came to my vestry in despair. The words tumbled out: 'I have gone too far this time. God will not forgive me again. Help me, Pastor. Is there any hope?' I asked him to go outside and measure up the chapel wall with a tape measure. 'When you have measured up to heaven,' I said, 'please come in again and tell me how far it is.' With immense disgust he retorted, 'That is stupid, absolutely stupid.' I replied, 'No more stupid than your assumption that God has run out of mercy and compassion.' He saw the point and was delivered.

In Jeremiah 31:20 the Lord says, 'My heart yearns for him; I will surely have mercy on him.' But do we, like the young man just mentioned, refuse to run into the embrace of our compassionate outreaching God, saying, 'Oh, I am so unworthy. I have gone too far'? We grieve and insult the Lord of glory by such unbelief, as though our failure could exhaust the capacity of his heart. 'The Lord's lovingkindnesses indeed never cease, for His compassions never fail. They are new every morning;

great is Thy faithfulness' (Lam 3:22–23).

God's compassion is wholehearted

Human abilities fail with increasing age. When I was a
young man I could carry two one hundredweight bags of
cement, one under each arm. Today two bags of sugar
are about my limit. Slowly but surely we all deteriorate.
A seventy-year-old man will not normally run a four-
minute mile. A woman's powers of concentration will
fade. Even a teenager will not necessarily remember all
he learned at college that morning. We engage in pro-
jects wholeheartedly when we first begin them, but our
enthusiasm wanes, and our ability to retain and recall
diminishes. We may care very wonderfully for a sick
relative at first, but after some years it is harder to
maintain this attitude of caring to the same degree. A
pastor may come to a church bursting with enthusiasm
and full of concern for the people under his charge, but
after a while—and a few leaders' meetings—his wholeheartedness could wane. In one of the churches in which
I served a boy sat in the meeting obviously bursting to
say something. When given the chance he declared, 'I
am going to be a concert pianist.' When I asked him how
often he practised he said, 'Five hours a day.' How
wonderfully wholehearted! Three weeks later, however,
he had decided to be a fireman!

Unlike fickle and finite man 'the Everlasting God
...does not become weary or tired. His understanding is
inscrutable' (Is 40·28). His interest in the sparrows is just
as acute as when he first created them. His count of the
stars is as exact as when he first adorned the sky with
them. His love for man and his ability to keep him is as
strong as in the days when he first chatted to Abraham.

When God forgives he does so with all his heart; he
even blots our sin out of his memory when we repent and

ask for forgiveness. When he judges he does so with all his heart. When he loves us he does it wholeheartedly. The Lord is not capable of halfheartedness, it is simply not in his nature, yet so many Christians believe that he is rather hesitant to bless or forgive them. What makes these people such special cases, I wonder!

God's compassion is attentive

God does not merely see men on the earth, he watches over them. David said, 'Thou dost know when I sit down and when I rise up' (Ps 139:2) and again, 'Where can I flee from Thy presence? If I ascend to heaven, Thou art there; if I make my bed in Sheol, behold, Thou art there' (Ps 139:8). God said to Jeremiah, 'Before I formed you in the womb I knew you' (Jer 1:5). In Matthew 10:30 the Lord reminds us that 'the very hairs of your head are numbered'. (In my case God must be good at subtraction.) Indeed, 'The eyes of the Lord are in every place watching the evil and the good.'

At this very moment you are under the close, compassionate scrutiny of a merciful longsuffering Father God who cares deeply for your welfare. If he cares for ants on the forest floor and sparrows in their nests, is he any less caring and compassionate towards those who are his heirs?

God not only sees but he listens. This goes beyond mere hearing. Children hear their parents say, 'Time for bed now dear,' but their lack of response indicates that they did not actually listen. Usually there follows the ministry of the laying on of hands, which often helps to clear the hearing! I have been physically deaf for forty years now, and it is a real nuisance. Whereas most people hear all day, people like me have to *listen* hard all day. It has taught me a great deal about the acute way in which God listens to every sound in the universe. He listens so attentively because he cares and feels for all his creation. Of course there remains the mystery of God's silence. If he hears why does he not answer? If he feels for me why does he not move on my behalf? With my present finite mind I cannot possibly comprehend all the answers to these questions, but I am learning to live in the context of eternity. If I believe that I am destined to reign in the eternal kingdom I will accept the rigorous training down here, which includes pressing on when God is silent; believing in his compassion when my mind screams out that he is cruel, and trusting that in heaven I will receive the full revelation of the mystery of God's will.

God's compassion is responsive

So far I have written a great deal about the responsiveness of God. I want to underline at this point that response demands response. If I show love to my wife I wish her to respond in love towards me. If I show compassion to her I wish her to receive it and appreciate it. We are made in the image of God; we have feelings, he has feelings; we feel, he feels; we need response and so does he. In point of fact the eternal self-sufficient Deity does not need anything. But in his grace and humility he has ordained that we can have the sheer joy and privilege of satisfying his desire for a loving response. This is fellowship and God enjoys it.

How can man, seeing a deeply compassionate God with extended arms, longing to enfold the disconsolate, still remain in misery and doubt, refusing the ministrations of the only One who can deliver and transform him? Can those who are rebels against the Most High still sin with unbowed head? Can those who grieve the Most High still persist in that which gives opportunity for evil powers to mock his sacred name? A response is

required when the Creator reveals his desire to men.
Those who ignore him will have to give an account on the
great Day of the Lord.

God's compassion is not sentimental

Although God constantly reaches out to us in wholehearted compassion, he nevertheless requires us to
humble ourselves and repent before he can comfort and
liberate us. 'Let the wicked forsake his way, and the
unrighteous man his thoughts; and let him return to the
Lord and He will have compassion on him; and to our
God, for He will abundantly pardon' (Is 55:7).

This compassionate fatherly God will still sometimes
watch us struggling because of our persistent sin and
stubbornness, and will not immediately come to our
rescue. When our children were learning to walk I stood
by to help them, but when they pushed my hands away I
stood back, even though I knew quite well what would
take place. Sure enough, they bit the dust. This did not
make me a cruel father—rather a loving one. My children
had to learn the hard way. When they were tired of
biting the dust, they stretched out their hands in entreaty
and straightaway I responded. Compassion is not weak
but strong. Longsuffering is restraint in the face of
provocation though punishment is deserved. That
demands strength, but our God is a mighty God.

STOP AND THINK

If God is compassionate then so must I be. If I have the
Spirit of God within me then I can be compassionate. If I
truly love God, I will be full of compassion. If it was
costly for God to show compassion then it will be for me
too. Everything worth while has a price to it. Pay it as an
act of worship.

3

A God Who Grieves

God is perfectly self-sufficient, in absolute control of all
things, and not in the least frustrated by man's intransi-
gence. Nevertheless, in some mysterious way he does
have real and deep emotions regarding everything he
has created. When we contemplate God we are dealing
with mysteries. I do not understand how God can be
filled with grief and joy at the same time, without imbalance. It is a mystery, but I must either accept it as
such or reject it and thereby reduce God to the span of
my own intellect. His feelings emanate from the depths
of his heart; they cause him to speak and act with great
intensity, as seen in the life of Jesus, yet they are totally
pure and held in perfect balance.

We all experience grief at one time or another, although the depth varies with temperament and circum-
stance. Grief is a deep-seated emotion and is not the mark
of a shallow person. Andrew Murray wrote: 'It is when we
feel deeply that we pray powerfully,' and those who have
known grief are able to intercede in a way that others
cannot. They experience the fruitfulness that may be
had through grief. Christians may be unwilling to make
themselves vulnerable to grief, but eventually this is
foolish, for great enrichment is thereby missed. Quite

23

frankly, we should ask ourselves just how committed we are to our God 'who grieves' if we try to avoid grief at all costs.

The Lord Jesus Christ was 'a man of sorrows, and acquainted with grief' (Is 53:3, Authorized Version). He 'learned obedience from the things which He suffered' (Heb 5:8). He did not walk through the streets of Israel with an impassive heart, but was deeply affected by what he saw and experienced. Grief and anger filled his heart when he saw the money-changers cluttering up his Father's house and cheating the poor. How dare they oppress the underprivileged and bring dishonour to his Father's name by their unrighteousness! Taking a whip he drove them from the temple courts.

The rejection of men also filled Jesus' heart with grief. 'He was despised and rejected by men, a man of sorrows and familiar with suffering' (Is 53:3). There was no self-pity, however, in his grief. He was not concerned that men rejected him as an individual, but that they were robbing his Father of worship and themselves of eternal life. When 'He came to His own, and His own did not receive Him' (Jn 1:11), it broke his heart because he saw them turning away to present misery and final damnation. Consider his anguish as he wept over the city, 'O Jerusalem, Jerusalem, the city that kills the prophets and stones those sent to her! How often I wanted to gather your children together, just as a hen gathers her brood under her wings, and you would not have it!' (Lk 13:34). With all his heart he called them, but with all theirs they rejected him. No wonder he cried out in grief, 'You are unwilling to come to Me, that you may have life' (Jn 5:40). If only they had. If only our unsaved friends and relatives would. If only they heard through us. How we need to see everything in the context of eternity. Jesus saw the whole glorious plan of eternal salvation, hence his grief when he knew that so many would miss it through their sin and unbelief. Do we share his grief over our unbelieving family or neighbourhood?

The Lord grieved over the sick and dying. As he walked this earth, 'In all their affliction He was afflicted' (Is 63:9). Jesus sighed in grief when he healed the deaf and dumb man (Mk 7:34). It was a sigh straight from the heart of the Father through the Son as they shared the deep needs of men and reached out to heal them. Jesus was 'deeply moved' (Jn 11:33), and wept (Jn 11:35) when he was confronted with the death of his friend Lazarus and the sorrow of his sisters. He was 'troubled' (Jn 11:33), which seems to indicate that his tears were tears of grief and anger. In Lazarus' suffering and death he saw the consequences of sin and was deeply distressed. He detected the hypocrisy of the Jews who surrounded the tomb, and was angered. At this moment he may also have foreseen his own suffering and death more clearly and the cost of salvation may have laid so heavily upon his holy soul that he wept.

Probably the greatest glimpse of God's grief is seen at Gethsemane and Calvary. That deadly cup, filled to the very brim with the wrath of God against all iniquity, was given to the Holy One to drink. He took the full force of God's judgement of man's sin, all his divine repugnance of evil and rejection of those who engage in it. He who knew no sin was made sin for us. Who offered that cup? Who made him to be sin? His own Father did. The sweetness of grace was entirely absent from that cup; it was unutterably bitter, no mercy assuaged its sting. Although Jesus was fully God he was also fully man, and in his humanity he could not even contemplate drinking that cup without being overwhelmed with grief. Confronted with the prospect of Calvary he cried out in agony, 'My Father, if it is possible, let this cup pass from Me' (Mt 26:39). So terrible was his sorrow, pain and revulsion that an angel had to come and minister to him.

Well might the hymn writer say, 'Never was love dear King, never was grief like thine.' Perhaps at this time more than any other Jesus 'offered up...loud crying and tears' as mentioned in Hebrews 5:7. If anyone would know the grief of God, let them ponder Gethsemane and Calvary more deeply. Jesus reveals to us a God who is far from aloof and impassive, but involved in our world at the deepest level. In him we see a passionate Saviour, overwhelmed by grief because of the sheer cost of redemption. It cost him his lifeblood! How is it that we can sell the gospel so cheaply these days and pedal an easy-believism. Do we forget his agony?

When we consider the cost of our salvation, it is hardly surprising that the unfaithfulness of the church fills God with grief and anger. Revelation chapters 2 and 3 unveil his emotions as he surveys his own blood-bought people. Their loss of real love for him, their toleration of sin (how popular the word 'tolerate' is in the world these days), their flirtation with immorality and the occult, their hypocrisy and apathy, all provoked him to speak out to them in the strongest terms. It was because his loving care for them was so great that he rebuked them with such gracious forthrightness.

God grieves over today's church as much as he did over the seven churches in the province of Asia. He still hears the shameful excuses of his people, 'Lord, I do love you. I know I grieve you but I'm only human. You must understand that I am weak. Anyway Lord, I love you. Receive my worship and forgive my sin.' Not only does this grieve God, it makes him sick. To the church in Laodicea he said, 'Because you are lukewarm...I will spit you out of My mouth' (Rev 3:15). Grief is never passive. In the case of Laodicea God removed the church from the earth. We would do well to remember that with the grief of God is mingled his anger. In Ephesians 4:30 we are expressly told not to grieve the Spirit. This proves that he is a sensitive person, capable of feeling grief. Scripture again points out that 'the flesh sets its desire against the Spirit' (Gal 5:17), so whenever we give way to the flesh we oppose and grieve the Holy Spirit. If only we meditated more upon the sensitivity of the Holy Spirit we might be stronger in our fight against the sin which grieves him and in addition we might escape the wrath which sometimes follows.

I believe that Jesus, during his days and nights of prayer, must have contemplated the actions of men, the state of the world, the terrors of hell and the feelings of his Father's heart.

So often and so long must he have done so that grief surely filled his own heart, but he did not sink into morbid inactivity. Rather, the emotions of his Father kindled his own with a continual determination to work in the light of them. Those times of communion on the mountains between Father and Son must have been utterly absorbing to the powers of heaven as they no doubt watched and listened. They were certainly essential to the work of the Son, for he plainly said that he could only do those things which the Father showed him (Jn 5:19, 30). What divine economy! If the Son of God himself required it, how much more do we! Seeing that God ordained us to be 'conformed to the image of His Son' (Rom 8:29), we should open our hearts to the Spirit of God, asking him to reveal his will to us. Those who truly pray as Paul did—'that I may know...the fellow-ship of his sufferings' (Phil 3:10)—will certainly share his grief as they survey the world with him. Furthermore their worship will possess that deep bass note which is so lacking in much of today's worship. Praise can be a lovely sing-song and may be the prelude to worship, but those who really worshipped in the Bible times were usually flat on their faces. They took account of the fact that they were in the presence of a feeling God. Their worship did not lack the minor key.

STOP AND THINK

Am I so blessing-orientated that I neglect the privilege of 'the fellowship of His sufferings' (Phil 3:10)?

4

A Joyful God

Have you ever seen some of the old pictures of Jesus, or
some stained-glass windows portraying him? I used to
see many of these while working for a firm of organ
builders. I longed to throw a brick through those which
showed him with a long, pale, miserable face and tears
flowing from his eyes. He would seem to be carved out of
putty or formed out of wax, and as weak and colourless
as those materials.

Now there is a difference between sadness and misery.
God certainly experienced grief but never misery. A
miserable God is unreal and definitely not the God of the
Bible. The God we see in the Scriptures has a vibrant joy
in his heart which showed in his face when on earth,
despite the trials he experienced there. I want to shout
with David Watson, 'My God is real.' He is a glorious
God, robust, mighty, vital, open-hearted, humorous,
and joyful with a great laugh in his heart. A zestful,
enthusiastic creator God. Angry, grieved, loving,
longing, yes, but joyful too. God is capable of experiencing all of these emotions at the same time, yet holding
them in perfect balance. This is a very hard truth to
understand, but one requiring our simple acceptance.

Joy is not the same as happiness. It is a strong vibrant
emotion, not dependent on circumstances for its con-

tinuance. It may not cause all of us to swing from the chandeliers, because God has made us with different temperaments. Some show their joy exuberantly and others very quietly, but whatever its expression, real joy is that which is embedded in our hearts as we go through trials and tribulations. Unlike happiness, which disappears when our circumstances are bad, real joy remains during the trials. When God says, in James 1:2, 'Consider it all joy, my brethren, when you encounter various trials,' he is pointing out that it is possible to do this, and indeed it is expected of a Christian. Jesus, 'for the joy set before Him endured the cross' (Heb 12:2). (I expect it was the joy of doing his Father's will and the joy of winning you.) This shows us that joy is always possible even in the toughest situations, and that is not an effervescent feeling but a deep strong emotion which carries us through the worst of trials. Perhaps the heights of joy are known through the depths of sorrow and trial.

Joy is derived. It is not a celestial commodity sent by angelic postal service to those who order a supply, but something communicated to our spirit by God's Spirit when we are close together. Joy is conditional. Psalm 16:8–9 says, 'I have set the Lord continually before me.' Only when we do the same will we experience the stability, security and fullness of joy mentioned in the following verses. Those who want the joy of God must learn to live in his presence where that fullness is. We will never find the time needed to sit before him; we will always need to make it. But surely fellowship with the King of all kings is worth this? Psalm 34:5 says: 'They looked to Him and were radiant.' In Proverbs 15:13 we read: 'A joyful heart makes a cheerful face.' (Christian, what about your face?) Again, 2 Corinthians 3:18 says: 'But we all, with unveiled face beholding as in a mirror the glory of the Lord, are being transformed into the same image.' The condition is that we look and the

promise is that we shall derive his likeness. If he is a God
of joy then I will derive his joy, and if he is a God of glory
then I will be glorious too. Isn't that what we long for
with all our hearts? Or is it something we merely wish
for? If the joy of God is worth having then let us go for it!
There is no doubt that we shall rejoice in heaven, but
why leave it all till then?

God is a God of abundant joy. He does nothing by
halves. If he judges he does so wholeheartedly as at the
Flood. If he blesses he does it with all his heart. Consider
his invitation in Malachi 3:10, 'I will... open for you the
windows of heaven, and pour out for you a blessing until
there is no more need.' Ephesians 3:20 says that he 'is
able to do exceeding abundantly beyond all that we ask
or think'. If he is such an abundant God then his joy is
abundant, and if he offers it to us why reject or neglect
it? Three men line up to urge us on. David says: 'In Thy
presence is fulness of joy' (Ps 16:11). Paul says: 'Now
may the God of hope fill you with all joy and peace in
believing' (Rom 15:13). Peter speaks of our 'joy in-
expressible and full of glory' (1 Pet 1:8). David exhorts
God's people to sing praises with dancing as an expression of their joy and glory in the Lord (Ps 149:1–5). The
joy of God makes us feel like doing just that. When my
sick wife is healed I will dance and shout with exuber-
ance, meanwhile we both rejoice in the Lord, sickness or
no sickness. We may express our joy more quietly than
others, but it is nevertheless a real joy.

God rejoices over you. Zephaniah 3:17 (Revised
Standard Version) says: 'He will exult over you with
loud singing as on a day of festival.' This both amazes
and excites me. I can easily believe that I make God *sick*,
but it is not so easy to believe that I make him *sing*! We
are correct in viewing God as the supreme Creator, Lord
and King, full of holiness and majesty but we must be
careful not to let this blind us to what he says in his word

about his attitude towards us. Few Christians believe
Zephaniah. His word 'exult' means to shout, be jubilant,
leap and dance, to be in high spirits. Can God really feel
like that about me? Some may say that God is speaking
to Israel not us, but if he felt like that about his earthly
people, how much more will he rejoice over us his blood-
bought people who are the Bride of his Son.

Many Christians spend so much time grovelling about
in the mire of their sin and in self-abnegation that they
fail to see the glow of sheer joy on their Father's face.
They fail to hear him singing in his great joy over his
beloved children. What a tragedy, and what a victory for
the devil. How much better to celebrate with God in his
joy.

God's joy is that of a Bridegroom. Isaiah 62:5 says 'As
the bridegroom rejoices over the bride, so your God will
rejoice over you.' Revelation 19:7–8 speaks of the saints
as the bride of the Lamb over whom all heaven rejoices.
It is because God sees Jesus in us that he is able to rejoice
like this. He is filled with gladness when he sees our
righteousness, holiness, obedience, faith and all the
other things which the Holy Spirit has been producing in
us since we were born again. I often ask congregations,
'Are you Christlike?' Their response is usually to drop
their eyes and to wriggle uncomfortably. When I change
the question to 'How many of us believe that the Holy
Spirit dwells in our hearts,' they respond readily in the
affirmative. I then say, 'Why did you have a problem
with the first question? What do you think the Holy
Spirit has been doing since he came into your life?'

All of us would acknowledge that we are not as Christlike as we should be, but if we focus only on the negative
aspects, we bring ourselves into condemnation which is
the first step towards spiritual paralysis. Moreover we
insult God by implying that he has not done much in us,
and we rob ourselves of the invigorating joy by which God

intends to strengthen us. 'The joy of the Lord is your strength' (Neh 8:10).

God's joy is a parental joy. Luke 15:10 speaks of the 'joy in the presence of the angels of God over one sinner who repents'. I would suggest that this joy emanates from the great father-heart of God as he receives another child into his family. When each of our three children came into our family we greeted them with real joy. Admittedly it faltered a little during teething, but we were thrilled to have them.

Parents have to cope with children's needs, tantrums, squabbles, and disobedience, but most of them still rejoice in their offspring. And so does God, who copes with millions of children. Sometimes he is angry, often grieved, but nothing prevents him from rejoicing over us and showing us off to his angels. It will help us in our Christian lives if we understand more fully the great fatherly joy in which God makes us his children (Jn 1:12), his heirs (Rom 8:17), and 'richly supplies us with all things to enjoy' (1 Tim 6:17). God says, 'If you then, being evil, know how to give good gifts to your children, how much more shall your Father who is in heaven give what is good to those who ask Him!' (Mt 7:11). The Holy Spirit surely rejoices to 'witness with our spirit that we are children of God' (Rom 8:16). I believe that part of the joy set before Jesus (Heb 12:2) was the joy of bringing men and women to his Father so that God could make them his children.

In the light of all this we can confidently rejoice in God's joy over us and shut our ears to the lies of the Enemy.

God's joy does not diminish, because he does not change: 'I, the Lord, do not change' (Mal 3:6). The suffering, corruption and injustice of this world undoubtedly affect him; the fickleness of his church grieves him, but he is not depressed or discouraged by it all; his joy remains. He looks at things from an eternal perspective, he has great purposes in view. His Son is going to reign over the entire universe, the world will be as he originally intended it to be, his people are going to be what he created them to be. The devil is going to be bound for ever, God's purposes will triumph. With all this in view, how can he refrain from joy?

As children of this God, our joy need not diminish, even in times of testing or pain. Jesus said, 'These things I have spoken to you, that my joy may be in you, and that your joy may be made full' (Jn 15:11). God always wants to share—his joy can be ours all the time if we really want it. Such a Christian is a strong one. His joy may not express itself in torrents of endless laughter or constant shouts of 'hallelujah', as though he had charismatic hiccups, but he will press on with God's work, despite its rigours, with a strong steady joy in his heart. He will have his eyes fixed on heaven with its prospect of God-glorifying rewards. These rewards are the satisfaction of knowing that he has been as salt and light in the earth; a comfort to the downcast; an inspiration to the discouraged; a menace to the Enemy; and the means by whom God saved others from the pit. Above all, he will have the joy of knowing that he has pleased the Father and will hear him say, 'Well done.'

How will he maintain this joy? Partly, as we have seen, by emulating David who testified in Psalm 16:8, 'I have set the Lord continually before me; because He is at my right hand and I will not be shaken.' The Lord Jesus himself endured and rejoiced in the same way. If our eyes ever leave the Lord we become easy prey for the Enemy and end up a miserable defeated Christian. And who wants a testimony like that?

STOP AND THINK

Am I joyful?

5

A Patient God

There is inevitably some overlap in the chapters of this book because it is dealing with feelings which are not experienced in isolation but together. Patience is an aspect of compassion but also a major feeling in its own right requiring a separate chapter and thus involving some repetition of previous insights.

God's grace causes him to be patient, he is gracious because he is merciful and in his mercy he shows forbearance. All these feelings and characteristics mingle together in his heart. Psalm 86:15 (New International Version) puts it beautifully, 'But you, O Lord, are a compassionate and gracious God, slow to anger, abounding in love and faithfulness.' Again, Romans 2:4 speaks of 'the riches of His kindness and forbearance and patience'.

God's patience involves restraint

Thank God for his restraint (why not thank him now?). How easily God could have destroyed Israel when she became stubborn, refusing to listen to his commandments and forgetting his wondrous deeds (Neh 9:17). Time after time she turned to other nations or kings for help when she knew perfectly well that only God could help her. Time after time she looked to her own resources yet God waited in his loving patience and restraint.

Why did she turn to other people or trust in herself for deliverance? Perhaps the answer lies in the fact that although God is only too willing to deliver men from danger and trouble, he lays down conditions for his intervention and in our pride and wilfulness we rebel against this. God says, 'Call upon Me in the day of trouble; I shall rescue you, and you will honor Me' (Ps 50:15), but we have to humble ourselves to ask for help and our proud hearts resent doing that. Again, God's ways are not our ways. We generally tell God how we want to be delivered and then howl until he does it. But God has his own ways which are usually very irritating to our flesh, though they are always the best ways. When Israel longed to be free from the Roman yoke she cried to God for a military messiah. Obviously the need was for a king with a sword in his hand. How else could mighty Rome be overthrown? There is no other way to smash a tyrant except by the sword. So ran their reasoning. Yet God sent them a carpenter. God's plan was to save the whole world—not just a nation. In Jesus he had someone humble enough to do it.

I marvel at the restraint of God both in withholding judgement for as long as his holiness allows it and in withholding answers to many of our fleshly prayers. In the time of the Flood, God withheld judgement for 120 years though the whole earth reeked in his nostrils with the stench of sin. He even sent Noah to preach to mankind for all that time in order to give undeserving men the chance to escape his wrath: 'The patience of God kept waiting in the days of Noah, in which a few, that is, eight persons, were brought safely through the water' (1 Pet 3:20).

In the face of human wickedness and rebellion, God

remains 'patient toward you, not wishing for any to perish but for all to come to repentance' (2 Pet 3:9). God is not a God of instant judgement but one who stretched out his hands all day long to a disobedient and obstinate people (Rom 10:21). I believe that God has restrained himself from bringing final judgement on Britain. For nearly a thousand years he has granted us freedom from invasion and a comparatively stable government, but we have taken his blessings for granted and turned our liberty into licence. Paganism and humanism are now the order of the day. Satan is succeeding in reversing God's laws and implanting into the heart of the nation that spirit of harlotry of which Hosea speaks. I tremble at this because there are limits to God's restraint. When the cup of Britain's iniquity is full God will usher in all his angels of judgement and this land will become another minor island. Let those who would question this, review the history of all empires which became rotten at the core.

In spite of this grim picture there is hope. If intercessors will stir themselves and do real battle against the powers of evil, if all God's people will gossip the gospel, and if we clamour for righteous laws, then the hand of God can yet be turned away from judgement.

God also exercises restraint. If God answered all our prayers we would either be spiritual spoiled brats or impossible to live with because so many of them are plain selfish. Furthermore the world would be in chaos! Imagine the different prayers from farmers on the one hand and holidaymakers on the other, or the differing prayers from various denominations. How wise God is to restrain himself from answering our every prayer.

God's patience is longsuffering

Longsuffering is the very opposite of the impatience, irritation and speedy retribution meted out by most of us to those who offend us. For how long do we suffer patiently those 'idiots' on the motorway for example? How longsuffering are we to those we love? If your beloved wife persists in squeezing the toothpaste from the middle of the tube instead of doing it the proper way (from the bottom of course), how long do you remain longsuffering?

Turn now and consider how long God has been forbearing towards us. How many times has he forgiven us our sins, restored us, and chastened us less than we deserve? Multiply our personal experience of his patience by the number of people who have ever lived and it will give us some idea of the sheer grace, mercy and patient longsuffering of our God and Father. It will also give us a mighty answer to the Enemy who so often tries to tell us that we have gone beyond the patience of God and can no longer hope for his mercy.

If God has persevered with man from Eden until now, then I cannot think that he will turn his face against those who read this book today. There may be some who particularly need to hear him say: 'Your sins will not exhaust my patience, I will not overlook them, but neither will I discard you because of them. My purpose is to make you great, both here and in heaven. I do not swerve from my purposes, nor am I discouraged by the weakness of man for I knew that when I saved you. Come now let us get on.' Remember that the One who speaks is the God described in Psalm 86:15 as 'merciful and gracious, slow to anger and abundant in lovingkindness and truth.'

God's patience reveals his courage

I do not think it irreverent to speak of the courage of God. For him to be patient with so many people through long centuries; to look at brute beasts such as Hitler, Stalin, and Khomeini with a heart of grace and a desire for their salvation; to wait for them to respond to the love of his Son and to hold back the full expression of his wrath upon such monsters takes enormous courage to my mind.

To remain longsuffering with those who have entered into salvation but persist in dabbling in sin requires courage too. His own church causes God as much grief as the godless society around it, for believers know that God hates sin, yet go on harbouring it in their lives. To take such people and mould them into the likeness of Jesus; to train them to reign in the everlasting kingdom; to entrust them with the precious gospel, and to give them work which even angels are not allowed to do— surely this takes courage.

How many times has God's boldness caused me to cry, 'Thank you, dear Lord, for your courage in training a wreck like me to be a king in heaven.' God spent forty years training Moses to be somebody, then forty years training him to be a nobody, and then he used him. Some apprenticeship! But what courage and patience God showed in taking this quick-tempered, self-assertive man and making him the meekest man on the earth, one who spoke face to face with the living God, and one who became a future ruler in heaven.

How wonderfully God copes with our human tantrums too, correcting patiently without crushing. My own father believed in the doctrine of instant response, therefore my tantrums were rather short-lived! Father's belt with his brass cap badge on it saw to that. The Cheshire Regiment lives on, imprinted on the anatomy of A. Buchanan! Its battle honours could include victory over his tantrums! But if only dear Dad could have been more patient, courageous enough to see that there was potential in me for a real heart relationship with him, how different life could have been. I would have obeyed him out of love rather than fear and we could have done so much together. God's courage, patience and longsuffering are meant to inspire us to love and obey him, to draw close to him and know his heart. May it do so in all of us.

There are limits to God's patience

Although God's patience is wonderful, nevertheless it does have its limits. His attitude of mercy does not change in the slightest, but there comes a point when he has to curtail human behaviour. God's heart of purity and love has no place in it for the kind of wishy-washy sentiment and spineless tolerance so prevalent today, reducing humanity to a collection of spoiled brats. God is training kings and priests.

God's longsuffering patience does not negate his wrath and judgement, 'The Lord is...patient toward you, not wishing for any to perish but for all to come to repentance. But the day of the Lord will come...' (2 Pet 3:9–10). Hosea, that great tenderhearted prophet whom I am looking forward to seeing in glory, gives a record of God's long patience towards Israel. He blessed them, forgave them, restored them and delivered them time after time, but finally he said, 'I will go away and return to My place until they acknowledge their guilt and seek my face' (Hos 5:15).

It is the most terrible thing in the world to lose the sense of God's presence with us. The only thing left then is to die, but even that is filled with the fear of his wrath. Some years ago when I was pastor of a church, I had an experience of this which has left a scar on my soul to this day. I had had an encounter with the Holy Spirit which transformed my life, but languishing for lack of fellowship in the Spirit I fell prey to the fear of man. I was told not to preach about the baptism of the Holy Spirit which I had experienced some time previously, and so I didn't, coward that I was. By refusing to preach the whole counsel of God, which includes the baptism of the Holy Spirit, I was grieving the Spirit. I was robbing God of his glory, and his people of encouragement by failing to acknowledge the great things he has done for us. My preaching lacked anointing, and I once heard such preaching compared to driving Pharaoh's chariot without the wheels on. It led me into spiritual atrophy and sheer desperation.

I took leave of absence and my wife and I went south to stay with friends. While there a faithful brother pointed out that I had grieved the Holy Spirit by not preaching the whole counsel of God. I was so deeply convicted that I rushed out into the garden and fell on my face under a tree where I wept my heart out. There I saw a vision of Jesus looking with sad reproach at me. It seemed as though my spittle was running down his face, for to be ashamed of him in not preaching his word is to insult him. I wondered if he would ever pardon me and I cried aloud for his mercy and forgiveness. Wonderfully he gave it to me with all his heart. He said to me, 'My courage is greater than your sin, my patience is more than a match for your disobedience. Rise up, your sin is behind my back. Come now, we have much to do.' When I returned to the church we had more blessing than ever before, and never again have I refused to preach the whole counsel of God.

Although God in his grace is wonderfully patient, we should not presume on this grace because it is meant to lead us to repentance not laxity (Rom 2:4). Paul asks us,

'Are we to continue in sin that grace might increase?' (Rom 6:1). The answer is a resounding 'no'. God's mercy coupled with his severity, his refusal to lower his standards to suit our flesh, his instant response to real repentance, and his great patience make him a God of hope and yet a God to be feared.

God's patience leaves room for hope

If nations or individuals reach the limits of God's patience does it mean that all hope has gone? Is there no further chance of forgiveness or restoration? I do not have a complete answer because I am not a competent theologian, but I can cite Psalm 103 in which God's mercy is described as greater than the distance between heaven and earth. Who has ever measured that? The Scriptures are full of examples of God's patience with nations, cities and individuals. In Hosea 5, although God says that he will go away from Israel because of their continual sinning, he does add that infinitely gracious word 'until': 'Until they acknowledge their guilt and seek My face' (Hos 5:15). Ninevah, that utterly corrupt city, reached the limits of God's patience but was delivered through repentance. Individuals such as Paul, a bigoted, proud, murderous persecutor who tried to wipe out the very church of the Son of God; David, a killer, adulterer, deceiver and warmonger; and many others could be said to have reached the limits of God's patience and mercy. God would have been quite justified in wiping them out, but he did not because he is 'full of compassion and is merciful' (Jas 5:11), and also because they all repented and sought his pardon—and found it.

James has some tough words to say to those who persist in sin, 'Cleanse your hands, you sinners; and purify your hearts, you double-minded. Be miserable and mourn and weep; let your laughter be turned into mourning, and your joy to gloom' (Jas 4:8–9). But he offers words of hope and encouragement too: 'Draw near to God and He will draw near to you' (Jas 4:8), 'Humble yourselves in the presence of the Lord, and He will exalt you' (Jas 4:10). Paul reminds us that 'where sin increased, grace abounded all the more' (Rom 5:20).

Although God is marvellously rich in patience and compassion, it is possible for nations and individuals to go beyond the bounds of his mercy. Although God cried out to wicked Israel who tried his patience again and again, 'How can I give you up, O Ephraim? How can I surrender you, O Israel?' (Hos 11:8), on the other hand he wiped out whole nations such as the Amalekites and the Amorites when their sins became 'full' (Gen 15:16). Hebrews points out the possibility that some individuals such as Esau can go beyond repentance and forgiveness (Heb 12:17). However, this should not blind us to the glorious fact that there is always hope for those who really repent of sin. Let us not waste our lives by dwelling in the cul-de-sacs of sin, but deal with it ruthlessly so that we may walk onwards with God.

Stop and think

Like Father like child. True or false?

6

A Yearning God

'Yearning' is derived from an Old English word meaning 'eager, intense desire, including a sympathetic desire to reach out'. It also means 'burning with passionate desire' as in 1 Corinthians 7:9, 'It is better to marry than to burn.' Paul's reference to his 'intense concern' (2 Cor 11:29) uses the same root. Perhaps intense longing with a degree of pain is the most accurate and concise rendering of this word.

God's yearning is intense

God's feelings are always intense, springing from the very depths of his heart. His yearning, his desire to reach out, to help, to embrace and possess is a powerful feeling expressed in many different ways. In his great longing for a righteous nation to honour him on the earth, 'He spoke long ago to the fathers in the prophets in many portions and in many ways' (Heb 1:1). Those prophets delivered oracles, or burdens, which were the desires that burned in the heart of God. In Jeremiah 31:20 the prophet cries out, '"Indeed, as often as I have spoken against him, I certainly still remember him; therefore My heart yearns for him; I will surely have mercy on him," declares the Lord.' God never gives up, his desires are too strong for that. His desire for a faithful Israel burns as strongly now as it did then and he will yet be satisfied by their obedience when the veil is removed from their eyes.

If God yearns over a nation, he must surely yearn over individuals like you and me. His deep and loving desire is beautifully portrayed in The Song of Solomon 2:14, 'O my dove ... let me see your form, let me hear your voice; for your voice is sweet and your form is lovely.' Such loving desire is scarcely credible. In fact, the truth will only move from our heads to our hearts if we meditate on it for a considerable time, but the effort is worth while. In the same poem the woman, representing the Christian, says of her beloved, representing God, 'I am my beloved's, and his desire is for me' (Song 7:10). This is another tremendous truth and one we should really try to grasp if we would live in the full joy of the Lord.

True love is always jealous love. Chapter 8:6, speaking of the passionate love of God and the intensity of his desire for us, also mentions his jealous love: 'Love is as strong as death; jealousy is as severe as Sheol; its flashes are flashes of fire, the very flame of the Lord.' A man deeply in love will brook no rivals, neither will he approve of any flirtation by his beloved with other men. However, his motives can be merely selfish for he is human, but God's jealousy is not of that ilk at all. His jealousy is a caring, protective emotion in which he, knowing that our greatest blessing and safety lies in being joined to him, reaches out to us with a strong appeal and turns fiercely against everything which would rob him of our love and fellowship.

God's yearning is possessive

Yearning to possess can be wrong and destructive for it can lead to lust, robbery, tyranny and covetousness, to name but a few. On the other hand it can lead to a happy marriage, a right pursuit of knowledge, and legitimate ambition. When we speak of God's yearning we speak of something absolutely pure. He yearned for a nation in order to make that nation great and to demonstrate how beautiful theocracy is and how wonderfully the earth would blossom when God and man are close in heart and thus close in working together. Indeed, this was his original purpose in choosing Abraham to father that nation (Gen 12:2–3). When Israel failed in her calling, God raised up the church and is now fulfilling his yearning by revealing his great wisdom through her to the principalities and powers (Eph 3:10).

God yearns for his church for this same reason. He yearns for you and me in order that we might be his heirs, rulers in the kingdom of heaven, inhabitants of eternity, those who share with the Creator all he possesses. He is jealous for us, he cannot bear that we should be robbed of our destiny. He is jealous lest we give our lives and love to another, his jealousy is not selfish, however, but springs out of earnest, burning care for us. He knows only too well that sin and Satan will corrupt and rob us, so how can he be unmoved when he sees them at work against us? God wants to possess us altogether, we are commanded to 'be filled with the Spirit' (Eph 5:18), and this means being filled with God. Why does he demand this?

I have heard it said that when God looked at his beloved Son he was so thrilled with what he saw that he decided to fill the world with millions like him. Although creation is beautiful—colours, trees, flowers, mountains and rivers making the world a wonderful place—God intended even more than all this when he created the earth. He wanted it not only to be beautiful but glorious. Even men can make beautiful things, but they can never manufacture glory because it is not in their nature. Glory is of the nature of God. It comes only from him and nothing else can fully satisfy him.

Adam and Eve were created to satisfy God's longing to reveal his glory on the earth through them. At first they were perfect, reflecting God's glory because of their close fellowship with him. But when they were tested they fell and no longer fulfilled God's great purposes on earth. However, God is never thwarted, and he gave himself in the person of Jesus to bring us back to himself and enable us to fulfil his yearnings.

He longs to possess you and me so completely that our lives overflow with the glory of his Son, Jesus Christ. In these renewed lives he finds tremendous pleasure, and through them he is establishing his glorious kingdom upon the earth.

A few years ago, God spoke to me in a prophecy saying, 'Give me a pure bride, a clean temple and a mighty army.' In those words I hear his burning desire for that which will satisfy his holy nature and will alone cleanse the earth. 'Be holy; for I am holy' (Lev 11:44), 'You are the salt of the earth... you are the light of the world' (Mt 5:13–14). Words such as these tell us of God's great longing for a people through whom he can change the earth. Blessed indeed are those who meditate on these words and listen to the heart of God. Blessed are they when they respond with that real love that causes them to yield their whole being to the Lord of glory. God-filled people are likely to create a God-filled earth.

God's yearning is steadfast

Many human yearnings are fleeting—intense for a time but waning when our attention switches to something different. A man may yearn after a particular girl, suffering agonies of desire for her. I did so myself over more than one, but when they did not show any interest in

48 GOD HAS FEELINGS TOO

achieving the dizzy heights possible to the wife of A. Buchanan I lost interest in them and turned to another.

God never changes. His desires remain strong and steady from age to age. His desire in Eden for communion with Adam and Eve did not disappear when they sinned. Instead he made it possible for them to remain alive by a sacrifice (Gen 3:3), then continued to watch over them and to commune with them albeit to a lesser degree. God never abandoned his purpose to make the earth a stage on which 'the manifold wisdom of God might now be made known through the church to the rulers and authorities in the heavenly places' (Eph 3:10). Nor did he close his heart to man, even though man rebelled against him. When God desires something he sets his heart on it and pursues it to the end. Angels must wonder at his grace to men when they so often reject his love, but they know that once there is a desire in God's heart it is there for ever. 'I have loved you with an everlasting love' (Jer 31:3), he says to us whose love for him is so fleeting.

God's yearning is undisguised

Although there are mysteries which God, in his wisdom, has chosen not to reveal to man, nevertheless he has made known a great deal to us. Creation is a revelation to man of what God is like (Rom 1:20). The rhythm of birth and death and the changing of the seasons are all designed to teach men something more about God. A regenerate man is shown even more, for the Holy Spirit has revealed: 'Things which eye has not seen and ear has not heard, and which have not entered the heart of man, all that God has prepared for those who love Him' (1 Cor 2:9). Perhaps the clearest thing God shows to us is his yearning for our fellowship. If the whole Godhead could endure Calvary because their desire was so strong for union with mankind, and if God bared his heart so wonderfully to us there, then it is the most heinous of crimes to ignore such a yearning.

God yearns for specific things

1 Chronicles 11:17ff relates the touching story of a much loved king, served by mighty and devoted men who were eager to extend his kingdom, not afraid of the cost, and who listened intently to everything he said. One day they heard him murmuring, 'Oh that someone would give me water to drink from the well of Bethlehem' (his home town). Immediately they set out to get it for him—simply because he wanted it. There were a few thousand Philistines in the way and the terrain was anything but conducive, but their king had a yearning and they loved him enough to go through anything in order to satisfy that yearning.

When they brought the water to him and he saw their dusty, sweaty, perhaps wounded bodies, and most of all their attitude of sheer devotion, he was so moved and grateful that he poured it out as an offering to the Lord. Some would have regarded this as a waste, as Judas regarded the ointment that Mary poured over Jesus' feet (Jn 12:3ff), but the whole point was that the king's men heard a specific request from his lips and they brought him what he wanted. Is that our privilege too? What then does God yearn for? If we can answer that question we will know how to bring joy to the heart of our King too. Let us find some answers to it.

God yearns for our heart

Perhaps God's greatest longing is expressed in Proverbs 23:26, 'Give me your heart, my son.' It is possible to serve God without your heart being in it. Many Christians, including ministers, are extremely zealous employees, doing all the right things in a highly organized way, but they do not work in that close heart-to-heart relationship with God characterized by the divine economy seen in the life of Jesus. Small wonder that so many break down at home and on the mission field. We have to be deeply in love with God in order to serve him best.

To be in love with a holy God requires holiness. A dirty, scruffy, smelly wife is not really likely to get very close to her husband and vice versa. Neither is an unholy Christian likely to get very close to a holy God, for sin is totally repugnant to him. 'Be holy, for I am holy' (Lev 11:44) is not just a command from God, it is a plea from his heart because he longs to be close to us. How can he share his heart with all its love, joy, and grief—its desires and plans—unless we are clean enough to be close? Small wonder that the Holy Spirit works so powerfully to convict us of sin, for that is the great barrier between us and our God. Isaiah 59:1–2 says: 'Behold, the Lord's hand is not so short that it cannot save; neither is His ear so dull that it cannot hear. But your iniquities have made a separation between you and your God.'

God longs for an obedient people. Obedience is a hallmark of those who love him. Jesus bore this mark, for he said: 'I always do the things that are pleasing to Him' (Jn 8:29). God could accomplish everything he desired through the loving obedience of Jesus. He could accomplish a great deal through us if we would only obey him. Notice that obedience is primarily a matter of the will. Our will combined with God's power gives victory: 'I can do all things through Him who strengthens me' (Phil 4:13). We are the Bride of Christ, and as such the Holy Spirit is jealous over us, longing to purify us, ever urging us into a more intimate relationship with our glorious Groom: 'Behold, all souls are Mine' (Ezek

18:4), declares the Creator, and his Spirit seeks to remind us of our obligation to be surrendered to him. We are the temple of the Lord, and the Spirit desires to take up his residence where he belongs. The NASB marginal reference to James 4:5 reads, 'The Spirit which He has made to dwell in us jealously desires us.' God yearns for his Spirit to feel at home in our hearts.

God yearns for intercessors

Ezekiel 22:30 depicts a man who stands in a gap in the walls of a city; a gap which should not be there, indicating careless sentries and heedless inhabitants, and a great opportunity for enemies to invade the place. It also indicates to me the deep desire of God to find those who will stand in the place of danger and plead on the behalf of others for mercy and deliverance. The fact that God looks for such and that he is willing to hear their cries shows that he is merciful and ready to respond if such people cry out to him in intercessory prayer.

Does it shame you to hear him ask, 'Could you not keep watch for one hour?' (Mk 14:37). My leadership of Intercessors for Britain is one of the most arduous things I have to do, but in the light of our nation's peril and the shortage of true intercessors it is probably one of the most vital.

God yearns for souls

Isaiah 30:18 says, 'The Lord longs to be gracious to you, and therefore He waits on high to have compassion on you.' 2 Peter 3:9 says, 'The Lord...is patient toward you, not wishing for any to perish but for all to come to repentance.' Again, Jesus said in Matthew 23:37, 'How often I wanted to gather your children together...but you were unwilling,' and cried out so poignantly in John

5:40, 'You are unwilling to come to me, that you may
have life.' Right back in the time of Ezekiel God was
saying, '"I take no pleasure in the death of the wicked,
but rather that the wicked turn from his way and live.
Turn back, turn back from your evil ways! Why then will
you die?"' (Ezek 33:11). All these scriptures indicate
the longing of God for men to be born again. When God
had to choose whether men should die or his Son, he
could not bear to let men die so he gave his Son who died
on their behalf.

God longs for heaven to be full, so just as the king in
the parable sent out his servants to the highways and
byways to bring people in to the feast, so God sends out
his Holy Spirit to convict men of sin and turn their hearts
to the God who yearns for them to dwell with him for
ever. How large is heaven? My answer would be: 'As
large as the heart of God.' When Jesus looked from the
cross down the avenue of history and saw you, he wanted
you and determined to have you in heaven, so he stayed
there in order to bring about the desire of the whole
Godhead. This desire was not merely for souls to fill
spaces but for kings to occupy thrones. In his great
prayer before his passion Jesus said, 'Father, I desire
that they also, whom thou hast given me, be with me
where I am, in order that they may behold my glory' (Jn
17:24). The greatest fulfilment available to man is to see
the glory of God. How wonderful then not only to see it
but to share in it. Indeed, one of the reasons God yearns
for souls is that they may share his glory. How strong is
our yearning for others to share such a destiny?

God yearns for unity

'Holy Father, keep them in Thy name…that they may
be one, even as we are' (Jn 17:11). This prayer is much
used by the ecumenical movement, but the basic mistake

which many sincere people within it make is to believe
that such unity is possible without agreement on the
fundamental truths which Jesus laid down. How can a
true Christian, believing as he does in the Deity, virgin
birth, atoning death, resurrection, and sovereignty of
Christ, have any real unity with those who do not share
these basic truths? How can a true Christian say that all
religions lead to God? Such syncretism lumps together
the heathen gods with the only true God who repudiates
them in no uncertain terms (Ex 20:3; Is 45:5).

The oneness of the Godhead which Jesus spoke of in
his great prayer was a complete unity of plan, method
and spirit, though each Person within this unity was
different and distinct.

Similarly, the unity which God yearns for among us is
that which binds together those who read and obey his
word, who walk in the Spirit, who may run their churches
differently from each other, but who love the Lord so
dearly that they say, 'Lord, I don't see things quite as
they do, but that's your business not mine.'

God yearns for worshippers

God expresses his desire for worshippers in John 4:23:
'The true worshipper shall worship the Father in spirit
and in truth, for such people the Father seeks to be His
worshippers.' He seeks them with the same intensity
with which he seeks to save the lost. There is plenty of
praise around today, but is it worship? What is the
difference between the two anyway? Praise is the out-
pouring of a thankful heart, the ascribing of greatness to
God, the exuberant rejoicing in a God whom we know as
Father and Saviour. It is both a natural response of the
redeemed and also an act of obedience to the Redeemer.
Psalm 113:3 says, 'From the rising of the sun to its setting
the name of the Lord is to be praised.'

A direct translation of the Greek word for worship is 'to reverently draw near to kiss'. Worship is an act which combines intense love with reverential fear, awe and wonder. It has a deep bass note to it. In Scripture we find that worshippers were often flat on their faces before God (Josh 5:14; Mt 2:11; Rev 19:4). When Duncan Campbell stayed with us in Matlock years ago he told us of the overwhelming sense of awe which gripped the hearts of those in the churches in the Hebrides during the revival there. What a contrast to the 'candy floss' pseudo-worship in many of our gatherings today. At one such gathering I was unfortunate enough to hear a girl warbling, 'O sweet lovely Jesus, O you beautiful thing, O you thrill me more than all my pop records, I swoon in your arms.' As no one was protesting I crawled over and tapped her on the head. Mercifully she stopped and I was able to say to her, 'Sister, remember it is your God to whom you speak not your latest boyfriend.'

God longs for our worship to be both truly reverent and truly loving. He is filled with delight when we express the deep love we have for him. Perhaps it is easier for us to envisage kissing the Lord's feet in loving homage rather than rising up and kissing his cheek in holy intimacy. Song of Solomon 5:13 infers that the bride has kissed and enjoyed the cheek of her beloved, and I believe there is nothing more Jesus wants than that our relationship with him should be as intimate. Consider the deep affection between John and Jesus expressed in John 13:23, 'There was reclining on Jesus' breast one of His disciples, whom Jesus loved.' Again, Zephaniah 3:17 says that God 'will exult over you with joy, He will quiet you with his love, He will rejoice over you with shouts of joy'. If God feels like this towards us, does he want us at a distance? We are the bride of his Son (Rev 21:9). Does the bride keep her distance from her groom? Does he not offer his cheek to her?

Much of our singing is just empty words. Some of those who roar in stentorian tones, 'We are more than conquerors,' cannot even conquer their irritation when the TV goes wrong. There is a great need for more reality and the leading of the Spirit in our worship. How much better this would be than casually saying, 'Will you lead the worship, brother?'

Another Greek word for worship is a word which can be translated 'to work' or 'to serve'. So our daily conduct needs to be just as much an act of worship as the celebration evening at the town hall. We worship the King of kings—let us bring offerings of worship which are commensurate with his dignity.

STOP AND THINK

Psalm 37:4 says, 'Delight yourself in the Lord; and He will give you the desires of your heart.' Can God delight himself in you and find in and through you the desires of *his* heart?

7

A Forgiving God

Whether forgiveness is a feeling in God's heart or an act of his will I am not quite sure. I do not find it easy to distinguish between his feelings and his attitudes, but even if forgiveness is simply an act of his will it comes from a God whose heart is touched by man's need and who joyfully responds to those who come and sincerely ask for his forgiveness.

Christianity is the only religion which offers forgiveness of sin. Most other systems demand appeasement in one form or another, either to satisfy angry bloodthirsty gods (demons in one guise or another), or power-hungry priests, before giving any hope of relief—and even that never materializes. These systems cripple man, holding him in a bondage of fear and offering him illusory benefits if he conforms to the system, but threatening him with dire consequences if he does not. There is not a glimmer of forgiveness, only a relentless demand for more and more appeasement.

God, in glorious contrast, is a forgiving God. Certainly at one time he required sacrifices for sin, but never human sacrifice except in the unique case of his Son. The sacrificial system he gave to the Israelites was not a cruelly devised system but a temporary measure through which their sins could be 'covered' until Jesus came to deal with them by that 'one sacrifice for sins for all time' (Heb 10:12). That sacrifice dealt not only with the sins of the Israelites but also the sins of the whole world, and opened the way into the presence of God for all those who would choose to come to him by it. Our God is a loving God who practised what he preached: 'Greater love has no one than this, that one lay down his life for his friends' (Jn 15:13).

All sin is against God

'Against Thee, Thee only, I have sinned, and done what is evil in Thy sight' (Ps 51:4). When we sin against each other, we sin first of all against the One who made the law which we break when we sin. God says, 'Love one another' (Jn 12:34), so when we act unlovingly we disobey his word which for the Christian is law. 'You shall not covet' (Ex 20:17), 'Owe nothing to anyone' (Rom 13:8), 'Do not lie to one another' (Col 3:9) are all laws which make us sinners if we break them. God laid them down, and we cannot tear them up without sinning against him.

The root meaning of sin is lawlessness or transgression (stepping over a boundary). It also means missing the mark. When we sin we step over God's boundaries and fail to come up to his mark or standard. Those who truly love God have his boundaries and marks etched on their memories by pondering constantly over his word as David did. 'Thy word I have treasured in my heart, that I may not sin against Thee' (Ps 119:11).

If it is against God that we sin, then it follows that only he can forgive us. If I smash up someone's car on the motorway it is no good my apologizing to the police patrolman. It is the owner of the other car who needs my apologies (and perhaps my wallet). Some denominations teach that they can forgive sin, but Scripture utterly refutes their claim by plainly saying, 'There is...one mediator also between God and men, the man Christ Jesus' (1 Tim 2:5). Only the one offended can say, 'I forgive you.'

Sin separates

A tremendous barrier stood between God and man after Adam sinned. God was still holy but man was not. God was light but man was now in darkness, and 'what fellowship has light with darkness?' (2 Cor 6:14). Amos said, 'Do two men walk together unless they have made an appointment?' (Amos 3:3). Adam's sin has both legal and spiritual implications. When he took the fruit from the tree of which God clearly said, 'You shall not eat, for in the day that you eat from it you shall surely die' (Gen 2:17), he broke the covenant that bound him to God in a perfect relationship. Isaiah 59:2 says, 'Your iniquities have made a separation between you and your God, and your sins have hid His face from you, so that He does not hear.'

Adam's act meant that God and man could no longer be friends, for sin now blackened every part of man's being. In fact man died spiritually, for as Ezekiel said, 'The person who sins will die' (Ezek 18:20). Colossians 1:21 says that we are totally 'alienated' from God, 'hostile in mind, engaged in evil deeds', and in Matthew 15:8 Jesus laments that 'their heart is far away from Me'. Man's condemnation is stark, awful and final. He is utterly helpless, 'having no hope and without God in the world' (Eph 2:12). Apart from an initiative from God, hell is the inescapable habitation for every sinner, for 'there is none righteous, not even one' (Rom 3:10) because 'all have sinned and fall short of the glory of God' (Rom 3:23).

'But God' (Eph 2:4)

These words are music to my ears even as I write them. What a phrase! I will sing it in heaven, I will teach it to the angels. It is as though the stars cluster together to spell it out across the universe on a dark night to counter man's despair. But even if they don't, the word tells us that 'God, who is rich in mercy, because of His great love with which He loved us, even when we were dead in our transgressions, made us alive together with Christ' (Eph 2:4–5).

'Christ Jesus came into the world to save sinners' (1 Tim 1:15). 'But now in Christ Jesus you who formerly were far off have been brought near by the blood of Christ' (Eph 2:13). He broke down the barriers, destroying the enmity between God and man, and establishing forgiveness and peace. I could weep for joy as I write this. Doesn't it excite you? I believe our dear God is excited about it still. I love J. B. Phillips' vivid paraphrase of Colossians 2:12–15: 'You... are sharing the miracle of rising again to new life—and all this because you have faith in the tremendous power of God, who raised Christ from the dead. You, who were spiritually dead because of your uncircumcision (that is, the fact that you were outside the Law), God has now made to share in the very life of Christ! He has forgiven you all your sins: Christ has utterly wiped out the damning evidence of broken laws and commandments which always hung over our heads, and has completely annulled it by nailing it over his own head on the cross. And then, having drawn the sting of all the powers ranged against us, he exposed them, shattered, empty and defeated, in his final, glorious triumphant act!' Jesus took on all that was against us—the wrath of a holy God, the condemnation of the law, the domination of the devil, our fallen nature and our terrible record of sin. At Calvary, that unique battleground, altar, hell on earth and court of justice, Jesus cried out, 'It is finished!' (Jn 19:30)—and it was! The offering was made, the verdict given, the curse removed, the battle won. Forgiveness was not only possible now, but freely offered to man if he would repent and turn to God. I found it myself. Have you?

Blotted out

Forgiveness means 'lifting away', and Jesus did this so completely that our sins cannot be found (Ps 103:12). God took them out of his memory and put them into his 'forgettory'. 'I have wiped out your transgressions like a thick cloud,' he says, 'and your sins like a heavy mist' (Is 44:22). Again, in Jeremiah 31:34 he says, 'I will forgive their iniquity, and their sin I will remember no more.'

I come across so many people who are tormented by their past sins. They have no assurance of God's forgiveness, they dare not look him in the face in case he is still angry with them. If only they would remember that 'the Lord has caused the iniquity of us all to fall on Him' (Is 53:6). All God's wrath fell on Jesus, so he cannot possibly have a lapse of memory when it comes to one of our sins, for that would be making Calvary incomplete. If he had overlooked only one sin, the universe would have collapsed before now. If the One who 'upholds all things by the word of His power' (Heb 1:3) had failed to the slightest degree, then God would have failed and therefore ceased to be the Almighty, and certainly could not have been a saviour. But there is no record of such a failure.

After sinning on one occasion, I went to God and confessed my failing. I then received his pardon and got on with my work as a pastor. Later on when I arrived home for lunch, I was assailed by the remembrance of my sin, so I went upstairs and began to confess it again:

'Lord, that sin, I ask you again, to for....' But I got no
further than this, for God clearly said to me, 'Alex, what
sin?' Then I realized the truth of his word: 'Their sin will
I remember no more' (Jer 31:34). What an immense
relief to look up again at a thrice-holy God—without
blushing. I turned, as it were, to that day's page in the
diary of my life and saw it white and clean. Then I took
great relish in beating the evil one over the head with the
word of my God: 'No more, no more, no more.'

So costly

To us forgiveness is free, but it cost the Godhead everything to bring it to us. It was the most costly thing in the
universe. It cost the Father his only Son, the Son his own
life, and the Spirit the agony of withdrawing from a
perfect man. Small wonder that there are conditions for
its reception.

Some years ago I had a vision of Calvary. Jesus was
hanging on the cross, gradually being engulfed in immense loneliness and great darkness, the Father slowly
turning away from him. As I watched in the vision, the
Spirit began to withdraw from the One who had never
grieved or hindered him. Vast hosts of angels were looking aghast as they saw this mighty drama played out on
the stage of creation. As the darkness increased, Jesus
was still looking into heaven, gazing up at his Father's
face, and still seeing the angels. But gradually the doors
of heaven closed, the angels turned away in horror, and
the face of the Father became grim as he saw his Son
'who knew no sin to be sin on our behalf' (2 Cor 5:21).
Then the doors clanged shut with a sound which
resounded throughout creation, the Father's face was
completely averted, the Spirit withdrew, the twelve
legions of angels stood unbidden, and Jesus screamed
out in sheer agony—the agony of hell itself: 'My God,

my God, why hast Thou forsaken me?' (Mt 27:46).

Many speak of the cost of the cross to Jesus, and of course no one can minimize that, but the whole God-head suffered there too. As the vision faded and we had finished weeping, I began to understand the cost of forgiveness, and began to have a greater hatred of the sin which made the cross necessary.

The way is open

When the Father saw that the plan of salvation was now completed, and the cry of victory came from the heart of Jesus (not a moan of pain but the death knell of all the forces of darkness and that which sent a shudder right through their ranks), God proclaimed that entry to his eternal heaven was now possible for all who would come. Jesus had given him the grounds on which he could forgive the sin of man without impugning his justice. To demonstrate this he tore the veil of the temple in two, significantly from top to bottom, showing that the barrier to the Holy of Holies had now been removed. God was saying, 'Come in all you who would share eternity with me, all may come boldly to this throne of grace to find mercy and healing.'

God's forgiveness is wholehearted. When he forgives sin it is not a grudging forgiveness. Luke 7:41–42 tells the lovely story of the man who freely and graciously forgave both his debtors. What a beautiful illustration of God's attitude. It is important to grasp this lest we should think that some kind of 'evangelical' penance is needed to complete our pardon. Psalm 32:1 points out that God no longer imputes sin to those who are forgiven. Psalm 103 says that he removes it as far as the East is from the West. No one has ever found the West Pole, though there are some introspective Christian 'explorers' trying to find one in their efforts to expiate their sins more thoroughly. What an insult to God this is. Far better to meditate on 1 John 1:9 and rejoice in the truth.

I found this poem a long time ago, and I am greatly looking forward to meeting the author in heaven and telling him how much it blessed me.

> Redemption.
> And what is this? Survey the wondrous cure;
> And at each step let higher wonder rise!
> Pardon for infinite offence! and pardon
> Through means that speak its value infinite!
> A pardon bought with blood, with blood divine!
> With blood divine of Him I made my foe.
> Persisted to provoke, tho' wooed and awed
> Blessed and chastised, a flagrant rebel still!
> A rebel midst the thunders of His Throne!
> Nor I alone, a rebel universe!
> My species up in arms, not one exempt.
> Yet for the foulest of the foul He dies,
> Most joyed for the redeemed from deepest guilt,
> As if our race were held of highest rank,
> And Godhead dearer as more kind to man!
> Leap, every heart! and every bosom burn!
> O what a scale of miracles is here!
> Its lowest round high planted on the skies,
> Its towering summit lost beyond the thoughts of
>   man or angel.

But there are conditions

God's grace is overflowing and he longs to pour out his forgiveness on us, but he nevertheless lays down conditions. How can he do otherwise seeing that our forgiveness is so costly? Although we are free to enjoy God's pardon, we must be careful never to take it lightly. As Paul said, 'Are we to continue in sin that grace might increase? May it never be!' (Rom 7:1–2).

There is a tendency in the modern 'charismatic' movement to take forgiveness very easily and to major on enjoyment. This often results in a lightweight Christianity and a lax attitude to sin. Conversely, the Puritans spent so much time bewailing their sin that one wonders whether they enjoyed forgiveness at all. The answer, as every tight-rope walker knows, is balance.

With these thoughts in mind, let's look at God's conditions. Firstly, God will not forgive the unrepentant. In fact, according to the Bible, 'He will sharpen His sword' against them (Ps 7:12). Repentance is primarily an act of the will, a change of mind leading to a change in direction. James 4:8 says, 'Draw near to God and He will draw near to you.' God has done his part and now we must do ours.

Secondly, we must confess our sins (1 Jn 1:9). This entails far more than the 'blanket prayer' in which we say, 'Lord, please forgive me for all my sins. Amen.' Such an attitude reveals shallowness of heart and does despite to Calvary. On the other hand, God does not expect us to squeal, whine and grovel before him, delving again and again into our wretched hearts to find one foul sin after another. God desires honest confession not a dredging into the murky depths of our being. Some believe more in everlasting introspection than in eternal salvation!

Thirdly, there needs to be a willingness to forsake sin. This is more likely to happen if we constantly contemplate the meaning of Calvary and allow this to produce in us that holy hatred of sin which characterized our beloved Lord Jesus who 'loved righteousness and hated lawlessness' (Heb 1:9). When seeking forgiveness we must remember that restitution may be necessary. Years ago, before I found real assurance of forgiveness, I had to return a complete tool kit which I had stolen from school. Then there were many apologetic letters to write and other property to be returned to the rightful owners. It was painful, embarrassing and expensive, but better shame down here than at the judgement seat of Christ.

Lastly, there is the plain statement from Jesus in Matthew 6:15, 'If you do not forgive men then your Father will not forgive your transgressions.' This truth is well illustrated in Matthew 18:21–35, and deserves our close attention. Could it be that we are kidding ourselves when we sing, 'I'm forgiven, I'm forgiven, I'm forgiven'? It is true that we are forgiven if we have been born again, but our daily record in heaven may be far from clean. Failure to forgive results in the break-up of families, churches and nations. It causes physical sickness, heart-ache and scandal, but perhaps its most terrible result is that it prevents us from maturing into a fruitful and effective Christian in this world and causes us to lose our rewards in the kingdom to come. How can God use an unforgiving servant? Far, far better to forgive, be forgiven, and get on again with the family business.

Father's nature

If God has such a forgiving spirit, so too should his children. When we received him he gave us the right and ability to become children of God (Jn 1:12). Again, 1 John 3:1 says, 'See how great a love the Father has bestowed upon us, that we should be called children of God; and such we are.' Peter says that we have been born again of imperishable (divine) seed (1 Pet 1:23). If we let this great truth sink deeply into our hearts we will understand not only that we ought to reflect the character of our Father, but also that we can. All we have to do is be willing to forgive, and to open up our hearts to the Holy Spirit who will give us the power to forgive. If we are reluctant to make the first move towards someone who has sinned against us, we would do well to consider those gracious words of Jesus from the cross, 'Father forgive them; for they do not know what they are doing'

(Lk 23:34). Remember that he was praying for those who had insulted, tortured and totally rejected him, finally taking his life. What a word of wisdom is found in Proverbs: 'A man's discretion makes him slow to anger, and it is his glory to overlook a transgression.' Forgiveness is more an act of the will than a feeling. Larry Christenson expressed this well by saying that when you decide to forgive one who has wronged you, you must remember that they are no longer accountable to you.

STOP AND THINK

If I have not forgiven others, how will I feel when I stand at the judgement seat of Christ, especially if those other people are also there?

8

The Wrath of God

One of the mysterious things about God is that he can be loving and angry at the same time. Human reasoning cannot explain this, but a humble Christian can accept it. God is too great to be fully comprehended and described by the human mind, but he is near enough to be enjoyed by those who are prepared to accept what Scripture says about him. Men can be loving and they can be angry, but one emotion has to make way for the other, they cannot be manifested together. Most parents love their children, but when the child persistently refuses to obey orders, anger takes over and the child receives the 'laying on of hands'. They still love their child, but the emotion of love has to make way for the emotion of anger for a while.

God is different from us because his nature is different. He is perfect, but we are tainted, twisted and limited because of our sin. His anger is pure, but ours is usually a hateful, destructive expression of grievance. Paul says to us, 'Be angry, and yet do not sin' (Eph 4:26). Anger is the only possible attitude God can take towards sin. He does not fly into a temper at the sight of it, but simply maintains his constant repugnance to it, his holy judgement against it, and his determination to deal with it. He cannot ignore it for he sees it wherever it is, 'The

eyes of the Lord are in every place watching the evil and
the good' (Prov 15:3). He must judge it because it mars
his creation (Gen 6:5–6); he cannot condone it because
he hates it. God's anger is always a just anger for it is
based on his perfect assessment of every situation.

How foolish it is to think that we can hide sin from
God. The psalmist expressed this well in Psalm 139:7:
'Where can I flee from Thy presence? If I ascend to
heaven, Thou art there...in Sheol, behold, Thou art
there...If I dwell in the remotest part of the sea, even
there Thy hand will lead me...If I say, "Surely the
darkness will overwhelm me, and the light around me
will be night," even the darkness is not dark to Thee.'
Even more foolish is the thought that we can escape his
anger if we continually and deliberately sin. Our knowledge of his anger and also his loving but sometimes
steely eyes should deter us from the sin which brings
down his wrath.

God's anger is an integral part of his love, for love
without anger is mere sentimentality. This combination
of love and anger is shown in Exodus 34:6–7 which
speaks of God's compassion and lovingkindness mingled
with his hatred for and punishment of iniquity. If an
earthly father is constantly giving and accommodating,
and always at the beck and call of his children, then he is
not a truly loving father. Hebrews 12:9 gives us a picture
of a father who can be stern and has no hesitation about
disciplining his children when necessary. Now this father
is truly loving and wins the respect of his children.

Years ago, as a prison visitor, I spoke to a man accused
of a very serious crime. He asked me if my father had
ever got angry with me and whether or not he punished
me. I said that yes, my father did both, and in fact he
punished me quite severely fairly often. This prisoner's
response was to shout at me saying, 'He didn't punish
you, I don't believe it, you are a liar!', to which I replied,

'Friend, I'm telling you the truth, my dad did punish me.' He shouted again, 'He didn't, he didn't, he didn't!' weeping copiously as he did so. When he had calmed down he said, 'Listen mate, I wish to God my dad had belted me, if he had I wouldn't be here now.' And he wept again. Thank God for discipline, whether it is from our earthly father or our heavenly Father.

We must always remember, however, that when God disciplines us he is never sadistic as some earthly fathers are. Many people have come to us with serious emotional problems, stemming in some cases from ill-treatment by their fathers. Boys have been scorned and degraded because they did not match up to their fathers' plans for them. Girls have been intimidated by their fathers, or kept at arm's length so that they never knew what a father's love was like. Similarly, sons have been unable to confide in their father because he was so remote. Many children grow up in an atmosphere of fear and tension, knowing all about a father's anger, but nothing of his love. Their relationship with their father affects their entire picture of God. To them he is a stern fault-finding being, with eyes like twin laser beams, searching for the slightest excuse to rain punishment upon them. An exacting tyrant who is far more keen to mete out judgement than shower them with mercy. How far this is from the God portrayed in Psalm 103:8–14. This passage is well worth studying by those who have been deeply wounded at home.

When we feel God's anger against us because of our sin, we should not think that he has stopped loving us. Hebrews 12:5–6 points out that it is because he loves us that he chastens us. Conversely, when we feel his love upon us in unusual measure, we must not think that he will overlook our need for constant discipline. God's chastening is a loving but very firm checking and redirecting. Perhaps an illustration will help. Years ago, when our daughter Ruth was small, we lived in a country town which had a park with a river running through it. When walking in this park, we would release Ruth from her reins and she would run off on her own, but always towards the fast-flowing river. I would call out, 'Ruth, not that way, it's dangerous.' No response, so I would call again a second and third time. Lack of response made me angry as well as concerned so I ran up and held her shoulders quite tightly. She struggled, screamed and squirmed, but I held on, saying, 'Not that way, dear, it's dangerous. Go this way, it's safe.' Angry? Yes, but loving too.

In life's experiences most of us learn the hard way. Many years ago, when I was a young man, I concluded that no one loved me and that my parents did not understand me. I made plans to run away from home and be independent. I got a flat and packed my bags, but I did not pray about my decision. About the same time, our Sunday school party was to feature a sketch from *A Christmas Carol*, and for some strange reason I was chosen to play Scrooge. During a scene in which Scrooge chases the office boy out of the room, the lad who played the part of the office boy slammed the door shut in my face with such exquisite timing that I suffered concussion for three days and was confined to bed. When I came to, I was furious that my plans had been thwarted, and on top of this I had a monumental headache. The more I raged the more I ached. After some time I began to feel that God was angry with me for planning to move without his permission, but this only made me more resentful. However, God prevailed, I stayed, and my concussion went. Only later on did I see how good God was to be angry with me—my life would have gone terribly wrong if I had done what I wanted to do.

God's anger can be really fierce when it is poured out in strength. Consider the story of Amalek who opposed

God by afflicting Israel (1 Sam 15:2–33). God's anger burned against him and his tribe, as it always does against the determinedly rebellious, therefore God declared war on him (Ex 17:16), and poured out his wrath on every Amalekite (1 Sam 15:3). I often wondered about the justice of this, until a certain experience I had as a worker in the building trade. I was shovelling tons of rubbish onto a lorry when I came upon a rat's nest— Mum and Dad plus several little furry horrors. Having seen babies die from rats' bites, and having heard of the results of diseases spread by rats, I did not pick them up, fondle or feed them, but instead used my shovel to beat the life out of them. Cruel? Not really, a baby rat grows into an adult rat, spreading disease and death as its parents did and its children will do after it. Similarly God saw that the Amalekites would not change from generation to generation, so out of sheer wrath against their sin and in his great mercy towards other men, he rid the earth of them.

Even God's own priests are not spared from his fierce wrath. Nadab and Abihu thought they knew better than God and disobeyed him. These men had seen the glory of God (Ex 24:9–10), they were elders of Israel as well as priests, and sons of Aaron himself. Nevertheless, when they gave way to pride and disobedience the wrath of God fell upon them (Lev 10:2). Ananias and Sapphira were born-again believers and founder members of the early church, yet when they lied to the Holy Spirit, God smote them in his fierce anger. Well might Paul exhort us in 1 Corinthians 10:12, 'Let him who thinks he stands take heed lest he fall.'

Yet God does not fail to be merciful. In Noah's day, he waited for 120 years so that people could repent and flee from the wrath to come. Noah preached and prepared a refuge. Through him God offered men freedom from divine wrath and judgement, including a way of physical salvation. Who can blame God when he finally opened the very gates of heaven and poured out abundant wrath. This should not engender terror within us, but bring that true fear of the Lord which is the beginning of wisdom (Prov 1:7).

There is a far more terrible manifestation of the fierce wrath of God against sin than all these incidents—Calvary, where God vented his feelings about that which had marred his whole creation, and dealt with it completely and utterly. The 'fierce wrath of God, the Almighty' (Rev 19:15) was to be poured out upon men because of human sin. No mercy was to be given, no compassion allowed; there would be neither reprieve nor relief. God would empty the vials of his wrath and not one drop would be left. He would execute absolute justice and then turn away his face, slam the gates of heaven shut, and leave the victim utterly alone, completely deserted, cursed with the curse of the law and consigned to the lowest hell. I tremble as I write, for that was my fate and just reward. So terrible was it that even Jesus sweated blood and needed an angel to strengthen him as he contemplated his ordeal in Gethsemane. And yet he bore it—'In my place condemned He stood, sealed my pardon with His Blood, Hallelujah, what a Saviour.' But oh the cost of it! 'Oh Christ, what burdens bowed Thy Head!'

It was the love of God which caused him to deal with sin like this so that men might fulfil their true purpose. It was the grace of God which let Jesus replace us. It was the power of God through the Spirit to bring Jesus back from the lowest hell to prove that sin's dominion was shattered and that God and man could now dwell together. At Calvary the whole Godhead was at work to restore man to his destiny. But what a cost. Yet we still flirt with the sin that brought God's anger down on his beloved Son. If only we meditated more often upon the glories of Calvary, we would find ourselves completely disgusted by that sin, and quite unable to have anything more to do with it.

Mercifully, the anger of God is usually brief in its manifestation: 'His anger is but for a moment... weeping may last for the night, but a shout of joy comes in the morning' (Ps 30:5). 'In an outburst of anger I hid My face for a moment; but with everlasting lovingkindness I will have compassion on you' (Is 54:8). If God refrained from anger his children would become spoiled brats having little idea of their Father's great holiness and showing little, if any, of it themselves. How could such people be salt and light in the world? They would be mere blessing-seekers instead of holy, sacrificial, reverent workers in the Father's vineyard. Teaching which represents God as a jovial and benevolent Father Christmas figure does nothing to produce rugged children of God but tends rather to make them spiritual weaklings. Such will never reign in life as overcomers, but will stay instead in a spiritual nursery. How precious is God's anger. Blessed is the hand that smites me, for it makes me great and keeps me in the paths of righteousness. Praise God, however, that he disciplines us in a way that we can stand. He chastens but does not crush. His anger is but for a moment.

Although God's anger is fierce and terrible, it can be turned away, but only by repentance and, where possible, restitution. The whole world is the Lord's and he has the right to do whatever he wills with it, but when people turn away from their sin, God in his mercy turns away from his anger and withholds his judgement. When Achan brought the wrath of God upon Israel it was fierce indeed. His own sin was too serious for his life to be saved, but when the nation of Israel repented as a whole, 'the Lord turned from the fierceness of His anger' (Josh 7:26). Again, when the wicked city of Nineveh repented,

God spared it, although in his anger he had previously determined to destroy it.

Human repentance is so often temporary or even partial. Asa brought great reforms to the nation and led them to repent before God (2 Chron 15). They made a great promise to God that they would serve only him, but they did not remove the high places (centres for idol worship) from the land. God responded as far as he could to their initial repentance, but because it was only partial he later poured out his wrath upon them.

Most of us have areas in our lives which are not really yielded to God and cleansed, 'high places' which should be destroyed. Such areas grieve the Spirit, hinder our testimony, and promote guilt, all of which may incur many a breakdown—sometimes even sickness—and inevitably bring the anger of God down upon us. Deep and true repentance is the only way by which these 'high places' can be torn down.

David Pawson quotes an evangelist who used to say, 'Don't come out to the front to accept the Saviour unless you are prepared to leave your sins on your seat.' Alas today there is an emphasis on simply accepting Jesus, leaving in many cases sin not dealt with. Although not all physical and emotional problems are caused by sin, a number of them are due to downright disobedience and a persistent tinkering with what we know to be wrong; 'high places' tolerated and not destroyed; remorse rather than repentance.

Repentance is a matter of the will rather than the emotions. Jesus said to the sick man at Bethesda, obviously a sinner (Jn 5:14), 'Do you wish to get well?' (Jn 5:6). In the same way God would say to us, 'If you are willing and I am able, let us join up.' To put it simply, my will plus God's power equals victory. Some years ago a friend asked me to help him with a difficult counselling case. A woman, recently delivered from witchcraft, was experiencing great difficulties and torments although she had professed conversion. As my friend and I prayed I saw a vision of her hands bound tightly with a silky cord. I concluded that she was bound in her spirit, but God beckoned me to look more closely. When I did so I saw that the end of the cord was held between her thumb and her palm. It was obvious that she was deliberately retaining her hands and therefore could not be free because she was not willing. Consequently, God's anger was not turned away because there was no true repentance.

If we really enlarged on God's hatred of sin and the anger he brings to bear upon it when we counsel people for salvation, we might have more of those rugged disciples whom God is seeking to wage war on the kingdom of darkness. Trying to extend the kingdom of light while flirting with darkness is to live in a kind of twilight. It is a contradiction in terms. As 1 John says, 'If we say that we have fellowship with Him and yet walk in the darkness, we lie and do not practice the truth.' How can anyone say that he loves Jesus if he does not hate sin? How will people hate sin if they are not properly counselled about it in the first place?

God desires a clean, pure church through which to establish his clean, pure kingdom on earth. He desires this so strongly that he turns his anger against anything which would prevent it. If we understood what those things were, we would surely turn away from them out of our love for him. In Proverbs 6:17–19 we read of 'six things which the Lord hates, seven which are an abomination to him': pride, lies, murder, wicked plans, an appetite for sin, perjury and discord. Numbers 11:1—13:31 speaks of the rebellion, envy and unbelief of Israel which provoked God's wrath. As God's anger was roused against those sins which soiled his chosen nation, in the same way it is roused against those things which make his church impure. But if we repent, God's wrath will abate, his Son will rejoice and the Holy Spirit will be able to cleanse and renew the world.

What an exciting prospect! A world that has been cleansed because we have opened ourselves up to God so he can make us as salt and light. A Saviour delighting in our fellowship as we increasingly hate sin and love righteousness as he does. The anger of God abating as he sees us preparing the way for him to be gracious to a world which only deserves his wrath.

STOP AND THINK

God will help me to hate sin which angers him. Shall I let him?

9

God Is Love

The love of God permeates and binds together all his other feelings, and so it is fitting to talk about this most important and fundamental quality last of all. God's love is not a spineless sentimentality, but a strong and constant attitude towards us which can stand up to the pressures put upon it by our failures and disobedience. Today's world would rather say that love is God, for this enables them to bow down and give their allegiance to an attitude of easy toleration which allows them to get away with anything they like. The world uses the word love to describe anything from putting 10p into a flag day collection to a homosexual 'marriage'. It has become a debased word and a distorted concept. How vital it is then for Christians to show the world what God means by love. We will only do so if we know God by continual contemplation of his word, and constant fellowship in prayer.

If you ask the average Christian to describe God he will usually start with 1 John 4:8, 'God is love.' It is such a simple word and yet I find myself struggling with a mystery as I contemplate it. I believe it, I rejoice in it, I am strengthened by it, and yet I think of wars, earthquakes, accidents, disease, and many other situations where God does not intervene. Again, there is the fact that a personal devil exists, spoiling creation, destroying

77

the bodies and minds of millions of people, bringing them into an eternal hell. Yet God allows all this. How then can he be love? I do not have an easy answer, but I would say that the reason for all these ills is not God's indifference but man's poor stewardship of the earth. When Adam exchanged his stewardship of the entire earth for the illusory promise of Satan that he would be like God, he opened the way for the calamities so rampant in our world. Satan still whispers the same lie to men today and they still fall for it, so the old calamities are perpetuated. God could have shut down creation at the fall if he had wanted, but you and I would never have been born. Grace, faith, patience, triumph over evil, love and forgiveness would never have been demonstrated to angels and principalities. God was not taken by surprise when sin made its appearance. He had been to the end of history and back again and foreknew (but not foreordained) what would happen. God had courage and wisdom enough to let all these things occur because of the good which could come and indeed has come out of it all. He 'works all things after the counsel of His will' (Eph 1:11), and causes 'all things to work together for good to those who love God, to those who are called according to His purpose' (Rom 8:28). I do not quote these scriptures glibly. My wife and I have been ill, hampered, tried and often frustrated for many years. We have prayed and fasted, many people have laid hands on us, hundreds pray for us, yet we are still sick and hindered. However, we have learnt so much and have seen God work so wonderfully both for us and through us that we believe ever more deeply in the truth that God is love, whatever the circumstances.

God is love

When John says that God is love, he is touching upon a deep mystery—God the Father is love, God the Son is love, and God the Holy Spirit is love. Now we can either spend years in frustrated effort trying to fully comprehend the Trinity with our finite minds, or bow down and say, 'Lord, I cannot understand but I believe.' God has not left us to grope in darkness, but through the Bible has helped us to grasp how the whole Godhead came close to man in order to show his love. The Father 'so loved the world that He gave His only begotten Son' (Jn 3:16). He gave what was most precious to him, knowing it was the costliest step he could possibly take. The Son loved the world so much that he was willing to demonstrate it—to the point of laying down his life. The Spirit loved the world so much that he empowered the Son to show this love, and laid himself open to be grieved as he confronted sin. Jesus said, 'He who has seen Me has seen the Father...I am in the Father and the Father in Me' (Jn 14:9–10), and spoke of 'the Helper, the Holy Spirit, whom the Father will send in My name' (Jn 14:26). The Father, the Son and the Holy Spirit do everything together. They are one in thought, will and action. They are love.

God loves the unlovely

Human love depends on finding something loveable in another person, but God loves the unlovely—although we were 'separate from Christ...having no hope and without God in the world' (Eph 2:12), 'while we were yet sinners, Christ died for us' (Rom 5:8). Isaiah reminds us that 'all our righteous deeds are like a filthy garment' in God's sight (Is 64:6), and Paul says, 'You were dead in your transgressions and the uncircumcision of your flesh'

(Col 2:13). There was every reason for God to destroy the lot of us; we were a stench in his nostrils and an offence in his sight—but God is love.

Real love is so strong and urgent that it has to be manifested. It shows itself in a constant giving out even to the undeserving, and perhaps especially to such. It is this kind of love that God pours out upon a filthy and undeserving world: 'By this the love of God was manifested in us, that God has sent His only begotten Son into the world so that we might live through him' (1 Jn 4:9). His love is all-embracing, at least to those who desire to be enfolded in it. He 'causes His sun to rise on the evil and on the good' (Mt 5:45). His heart is open to all. In order to understand the wonder of this we need to examine our attitude to those whom we most dislike, our greatest enemy, the most wicked tyrant who ever lived. We should then meditate on the fact that God loves them with a wholehearted love and longs for their welfare. Can we love them like that? Yes we can, but only through 'the love of God...poured out within our hearts through the Holy Spirit who was given to us' (Rom 5:5). This is divine love shown pre-eminently by Jesus who, in his agony prayed for his enemies, those who killed him, 'Father forgive them' (Lk 23:34). God does indeed love the unlovely, and with what love!

God's love is wholehearted

God is a God of abundance who does nothing by halves. But how few Christians believe in the wholeheartedness of his love to us. When the Spirit tries to do his great work by showing us the love of God, he is met with the protestation that we are unworthy and undeserving of it. Some believe that God loves them a little, but as for revelling in his love, that is only for supersaints. How we grieve God when we reject his love. He is not capable of two kinds of love—one sort for mature believers and another for struggling saints. His love is wholehearted and impartial. To shun it is a crime, to understand it is a miracle (happily performed by the Spirit), and to bask in it is life and health and peace. While meditating years ago on John 17:28, I saw in a vision the Father looking at his Son with all his wholehearted love and delight; then the Father turned his face—without changing expression —to gaze upon me. Then I understood, received, and rejoiced in the fact that he does not have two kinds of love. That verse came alive for me as I realized that the Father loved me as he loved his Son.

My wife Peggy and I often minister to the deaf with the Deaf Christian Fellowship. On one occasion Peggy was speaking to the women and trying to explain the sheer extravagance of God's love, but there was no sign in the deaf language for extravagance. Then an inspiration struck and she said to them, 'If I invited you for tea and gave you bread and jam with a cup of tea, sure enough I would have given you your tea, but if I wanted to show how much I cared for you I would have given you peaches and cream and a gateau.' They grasped the point, and ever afterwards they would talk about 'our loving peaches-and-cream God', or 'our gateau God'.

If we tend to reject such extravagant love on the grounds of our unworthiness, let us remember that God has chosen to love us and that 'He has clothed me with the garments of salvation. He has wrapped me with a robe of righteousness' (Is 6:10). These have made me beautiful in his sight. Some years ago I took a wedding at which the bride was hardly a raving beauty, rather the reverse in fact. But when she came through the door and down the aisle I was completely taken aback by her radiance and beauty, so much so that I seriously wondered if I was about to marry the wrong woman to the trembling groom. I thought to myself, 'If this is really

her, what on earth has happened? Why is she so lovely?'
Then I realized that it was her wedding dress which had
made the difference. Similarly, it is our 'wedding garment' given to us by God which makes the difference to
us in his sight.

God has also given us the divine nature, therefore he
can say in these beautiful words from The Song of
Solomon 4:9 (AV), 'Thou hast ravished my heart, my
sister, my spouse.' For me this poem contains some of the
most staggering verses in Scripture as it portrays the love
story between Christ and his church. Paul compares the
relationship between husband and wife to that between
Christ and the church (Eph 5:25–27). Hebrews 12:2
speaks of Jesus 'who for the joy set before Him endured
the cross'. Surely part of that joy was having us for his
bride. His great longing for visual, loving union is further
expressed in John 17:21 when he prays that believers
'may all be one; even as Thou, Father, art in Me, and I in
Thee, that they also may be in us' (Jn 17:21).

God's love is costly

It cost God everything he had to show us his love. True
love always has the hallmark of sacrifice. God 'did not
spare His own Son, but delivered Him up for us all'
(Rom 8:32). He did this willingly, not grudgingly, and
not because he did not feel for his Son, but because he
had decided to give everything he had in order to release
us from sin and judgement so that we might live with him
for ever. If we meditated on the verse: 'He made Him
who knew no sin to be sin on our behalf, that we might
become the righteousness of God in Him' (2 Cor 5:21),
we would gain a deeper understanding of the cost of
God's love, and this in turn would cause us to reject the
Enemy's whispers when he says that God places no value
on us. Jesus himself said, 'Greater love has no one than

this, that one lay down his life for his friends. You are
My friends...' (Jn 15:13). If it costs me a great deal to
love another person, I should look again at Calvary and
consider the cost of God's love for me, remembering his
words, 'Love one another, just as I have loved you' (Jn
15:12).

God's love is sensitive

A man deeply in love is vulnerable. A slight, real or
imagined, can slay him; a response can elate him. He will
not take kindly to a rival for his intended bride, nor will
he be unmoved if he sees his beloved responding to that
man. Genuine love is a most sensitive quality.

Now I want to be very careful in likening God's sensitivity to man's. God is not mercurial in his feelings as
men are, but he is sensitive. I cannot believe that God is
unmoved when we do not respond to his love, and when
we grieve and frustrate his Holy Spirit within us. Even
when we are responsive it is often transitory. God notices
when we are unresponsive or when our love cools and he
is deeply affected by it. Israel became bored with God's
love and frequently turned to other gods in whose orgi-
astic worship they seemed to find a greater excitement
and satisfaction. If only they had considered more carefully the feelings of the One whom they spurned and
grieved, and who cried out to them, 'What shall I do with
you, O Ephraim? What shall I do with you, O Judah?
For your loyalty is like a morning cloud, and like the dew
which goes away early' (Hos 6:4).

We would do well to meditate more frequently and
carefully on the sensitivity of God's love, for he is just as
heartbroken when Christians sin as when Israel did.
'The eyes of the Lord are in every place, watching the
evil and the good' (Prov 15:3). The state of his own
church is not hidden from him, and when he sees her

flirting with sin it must bring him enormous pain. What a crime it is to grieve such a tender, sensitive God by breaking those sacred vows of love and loyalty we made when we first knew him. Dr Jowett wrote, 'Sin, in the last analysis, is infidelity to love.' In the world such sin is commonplace, but in the church it should surely be rare.

God's love is jealous

Genuine and sensitive love is necessarily jealous love. God loves us with all his heart, and has the right to the whole of our hearts in return. In Exodus 34:14 he says, 'You shall not worship any other god, for the Lord, whose name is Jealous, is a jealous God.' It is possible for us to give God the whole of our hearts, for he never requires the impossible of us. His Spirit within us is love, and he wants to enable us to respond wholeheartedly to the Father; he is only limited by our will.

We should remember that love not only affects our emotions but also our will and actions. 'God so loved the world, that He gave...' (Jn 3:16); by an act of his will God decided to demonstrate the love of his heart. When our will combines with the power of God at work within us, then a right response comes about. A handy little equation to help us remember this truth is: 'My will plus God's power equals victory.'

In Matthew 22:37 Jesus commands us to love God with all our heart, soul and mind. This is both a demand and an intense appeal in which the desire of a jealous and holy God is made manifest. He does not utter a sentimental plea for attention, but demands that we make no covenant with his enemies and smash the altars to strange gods in our hearts (Ex 34:12–17). Anything that robs God of his rightful place in our lives and denies him glory has to be rooted out and destroyed. We may not keep images of idols in our homes, but our hearts could well be full of them. In a prophecy God gave me he said, 'I will not shuffle on to a section of the throne of your heart, I will not share it with any rival. Do not insult me by offering me a little bit of that throne, but show your love by casting out all rivals to my supremacy, then my angels will say, "O God, your people truly love you."'

I want to stress yet again the difference between God's jealousy and man's. A jealous lover is a potential murderer if he comes across a rival. His jealousy is a mixture of suspicion and envy, his desire is to crush all opposition, and his motives stem from selfishness. Not so our pure-hearted God. His motives are utterly right, for his jealousy is divine. A friend of mine, before his conversion, was courting a girl when he discovered that another man was attempting to woo her too. He waited outside the pub till his rival emerged, seized him by the hair, dragged him across some fields and through a hedge or two, dunked him in a slimy pond and kept his head under with his boot until the rival promised to leave the girl alone. All rather drastic, and certainly not in the courting manuals, but he was consumed with jealousy. If we would deal as drastically with all that makes God jealous we would show the world what true love is. And isn't that our calling?

God's love is demanding

When God seeks after us it is not for casual acquaintance but a relationship that is more intimate and binding than any other, in whch we offer him all the love and loyalty in our hearts. That is why Jesus asked Peter, 'Do you love me?' (Jn 21:17), rather than asking him whether he esteemed him as a friend.

Many people pretend friendship with God, saying that they believe in him, but God does not commit himself to them because he knows their hearts and that they are not born again. During Jesus' ministry on earth, 'when he was in Jerusalem at the Passover, during the feast, many believed in His name, beholding His signs which He was doing. But Jesus, on His part, was not entrusting Himself to them, for He knew all men...He Himself knew what was in man' (Jn 2:23–24).

Denis Clark of Worthing, one of my dearest friends and one to whom I owe so much, once wrote a book which no one would publish because of its title and main tenet of thought. He called this book *Evangelical But Lost*. He may have overstated things, but nevertheless it is possible to have all the evangelical jargon right, to have a thorough intellectual grasp of evangelical doctrine, to go to church, to give mental assent to that doctrine, even to say that we love God, and yet fall far short of his desire for a deep love relationship characterized by obedience to his holy word. In the marriage service the lovely words 'till death us do part' appear. Marriage, like the relationship between God and the Christian, is a sacred covenant of love. Our protestations of love are merely words if we are evading the loving demands of our faithful God.

Jesus' words are searching, 'Why do you call Me, "Lord, Lord," and not do what I say?' We are commanded to love one another, and if we do this we show that we love God, but 'the one who says he is in the light and yet hates his brother is in the darkness until now' (1 Jn 2:9). Hebrews 12:15 advises us, 'See to it that...no root of bitterness springing up causes trouble, and by it many be defiled,' yet how many churches are split by this sin. One such church had two of its members locked in a bitter dispute over land ownership, and as a result the church languished and virtually died. Then the Spirit of God quickened the above scripture to one of the disputants, while at the same time the other person was convicted by the words of Jesus, 'Do you love Me?' They both saw that their testimony had been badly damaged by their bitterness, so they set off to ask forgiveness from one another. They met halfway over the very land about which they were quarrelling, knelt down and sought forgiveness, which was immediately forthcoming, and embraced in real Christian love. At the morning service afterwards there were memorable scenes and genuine worship. One who was there testified, 'There was a light in heaven upon us and we were bathed in the love of God.' When God's loving demands are met real love is shown.

Perhaps if we preached a whole gospel we would see people completely surrendered and devoted to the will of God which is the wholehearted response to that gospel. Such a response was seen some years ago from a participant in a tour of Israel who asked for help in finding God. The counselling session was not very ortho-dox and went as follows: 'First, if you and I drop dead I will be in heaven and you will be in hell. Secondly, you have broken God's law and you must beg for mercy which I know he longs to give you. Thirdly, God demands your total surrender, lock, stock, and barrel. Fourthly, you can only serve God properly if you are filled with the power of his Holy Spirit. So please yourself what you do.' He laughed, wept, and then poured out his heart to the Lord in stumbling prayer. He then turned to me and said, 'Did you say total surrender?' to which I replied, 'Yes, nothing less.' He then said, 'OK, Lord, total it is,' and was soundly born again. Afterwards he said to me, 'It is so right to give God the lot, for he gave the lot for me.' Amen to that!

God is not demanding because he is selfish, but because he is wise and good. He knows that our love needs testing and it is for our sakes that he applies his tests, otherwise we might think that we truly love him whereas we may only be sentimentally attached. Our demands are often selfish and wrong, but those of God are always unselfish because he knows that obedience to them brings our highest good and greatest joy. His love can withstand our perversity for it is 'as strong as death' (Song 8:6).

The love of God is meant to thrill us, to strengthen us, to motivate us and cause us to obey him. It is meant to lead us into the very heart of the Lord and to satisfy the deep needs of our own hearts, for true love is reciprocated by love. I know that I am deeply in love with God, and I also know that he is deeply and lovingly committed to me. In this I find my joy, security and reason for living.

STOP AND THINK

Do I find *my* security and reason for living in my relationship with God?

IO

Privileged to Share

It is perilously easy to become hardened in our Christian
life if we are not careful. The rising tide of evil in the
world, rampant selfishness and self-seeking, global
tragedy brought to our lounge every day through TV,
and all the personal pressures of life can make us insensi-
tive to the needs of others and deaf to the cries of a lost
world. Our spirit can become so anaesthetized that we
are completely insensible to the feelings of our Father. Is
there anything we can do to change such a bad condition?
Yes, there is!

Firstly, we should reflect on the truth that we have
been chosen to experience and express the feelings of
God. Paul speaks of this breathtaking truth in 1 Corinthians 2:9–13. Just think what it means to be the confi-
dants of the Almighty. If this seems too wonderful to be
true we should remember that our destiny is to become
like Jesus (Rom 8:29) who was God's confidant (Jn 5:19,
30), and if this was true of him then it can and must be of
us.

Secondly, we should remember that because we share
in his nature and his Holy Spirit dwells within us, we are
able to share in his feelings too. 1 Corinthians 2:14 says
that 'a natural man does not accept the things of the
Spirit of God; for they are foolishness to him, and he

cannot understand them, because they are spiritually appraised', but 'if any man is in Christ, he is a new creature' (2 Cor 5:17) and he therefore has a new ability to understand and enter into the heart of God who is now his Father. If we really love God we will be eager and open for the Holy Spirit to impart to us the 'hidden wisdom' of God (1 Cor 2:7) so that we may sense what is in his heart and fulfil his desires on earth. If we deliberately harden our hearts to the feelings of God then we sin, as James makes clear: 'To one who knows the right thing to do, and does not do it, to him it is sin' (Jas 4:17).

We need to stir ourselves then so that we are able to fulfil God's intense desire to complete the plan of the ages. Feelings cannot be static, they must issue in action, and if we are willing to be stirred then the Spirit is only too willing to do so within us. His great work is threefold, to convict and bring us to the new birth, to set us apart and make us holy, and to empower us as Jesus said in Luke 24:49. When he has done this he can begin to kindle and excite us with the prospect of his doing 'exceeding abundantly beyond all that we ask or think, according to the power that works within us' (Eph 3:20), and make us those feeling people whom he can use to change the world.

Part of the Spirit's work is to lead us to meditate on God's word. No one can enter into the depths of God unless he returns to this old but neglected discipline. God will not throw his feelings and desires to us like spiritual Smarties. We must learn to sit down with God, having the word open before us, then pondering how he feels about our unsaved friends, our neighbourhood, our government. Realizing how deeply God cares will surely stir us into action.

The Spirit will also enable us to pray about these things in accordance with God's will and feelings. As we persevere in this great privilege and discipline of prayer, the Spirit will soon show us that the crying need of our day is that of revival, and revival comes when pure men care deeply about God's emotions then pray and act accordingly.

In this whole area of God's feelings and our part in them, we should remember that we have been chosen and called to be made like Jesus Christ. The Father said of Jesus, 'This is My beloved Son, with whom I am well-pleased' (Mt 17:5); if it pleases God to see his Son, let us please our Father by emulating his Son. If Jesus felt and demonstrated the Father's feelings and character, then let me do the same. Let his love, anger, compassion, joy, grief, patience, yearning and forgiveness flow into and out through me.

1 John 4:17 says, 'In this world we are like him' (New International Version). While we were living in York, my dear wife and I were praying one day and she said, 'Lord, please make us Jesus in York.' A brief, dynamic and utterly scriptural prayer, and one which God loves to answer. Indeed, he did so for Peggy, for one Sunday as we came up the aisle arm-in-arm from the communion table, a man was sitting in the front pew full of bitterness and rebellion against God. We did not speak to him, but he rushed out for prayer and returned to the Lord. The reason he gave was simply this: 'I saw a woman who looked so like Jesus that God convicted me and used her to bring me back to himself.'

Wherever Jesus went he caused a commotion. He was the light of God, the salt of the earth, the enemy of hypocrites, the dispeller of darkness, the exposer of corruption, the scourge of tyrants. He was splendidly intolerant of evil, openly scornful of pretence, a fearless denouncer of all who opposed God, and a friend of sinners. Isn't that a testimony to be desired? A path to be followed? If it was the path the Master trod, should not his servants tread it still?

I want now to draw some conclusions from the things that I have written in this book, and to point out that they are not pietistic or unrealistic. We should not suppose that sharing in God's emotions is like floating dreamily in a glorious bubble bath of wonderful feelings. Far from it. For those who choose to enter into the heart of God are choosing one of the most demanding courses open to the Christian. When Pharaoh asked his tutor to show him a quick way to learn maths the tutor apparently said, 'Sire, there is no royal road to learning.' He was talking about an earthly pursuit, we are talking about fellowship with the Maker of heaven and earth. Indeed there is no short cut to the maturity required to share the secrets of eternity. It is a hard and narrow road, but a royal road, for it is a road trodden only by God's kings and queens, and King Jesus before them. We cannot expect an easy life if we tread this road, but we can have a gloriously fulfilling one.

If we really believe that our God is a feeling God who desires to express and impart his feelings; if we really believe that in his Son those feelings were most tangibly and powerfully demonstrated; if we really believe that by the power of the Holy Spirit we can partake of the nature of his Son, thus sharing in his feelings and touching the world with them, then surely we will put our hand in his and say, 'Lord, let us run together'? If this is our heartfelt prayer and desire, then here are some important considerations:

▶ Confess any hardness of heart and failure to share God's emotions.
▶ Ask for divine sensitivity.
▶ Prepare for rigorous training by the Holy Spirit.
▶ Learn to 'consider it all joy' (Jas 1:2).
▶ Start to meditate on those scriptures which show God's feelings.

▶ Learn to think about your loved ones and your neighbourhood with him.
▶ Remember that even Jesus received training (Heb 2:17–18).

If we walk in the Spirit we will never be bored; his rigorous training and conviction will see to that. He will open up the Scriptures to us, sharing the deep mysteries hidden in the heart of God (1 Cor 2:9–16). All these mysteries are exciting, for God is a vital, enthusiastic, creative, and all-powerful person. How could walking with him possibly be boring? The Holy Spirit will lead us into considering every aspect of this world—from the condition of our next-door neighbour to the future reign of his Son—in the light of God's feelings about them. He will invite us to share those feelings and to allow them to shape our lives. He will show us how to alter those things that grieve him, and how to enjoy those that please him.

Anyone who has been born again of the Spirit of God can only be satisfied by spiritual things. It is often said that in every one of us there is a God-shaped void which only God can fill. In Ecclesiastes 3:11 we read that God has set eternity in man's heart. If we walk in the flesh we are deceiving ourselves, and ultimately face frustration, meaninglessness and despair. Only eternal, spiritual things can ever satisfy man. Jesus came to show us the new and living way whereby we can turn from the flesh to the Spirit, from the temporal to the eternal, from the small ambitions of this world to the great purposes of God for us in both this life and the next. Jesus is the One who pre-eminently knows and shares the feelings of his Father. He is also the One who gives us his Spirit so that we may share those feelings and live a victorious life that is more and more like his.

If we are conquerors in this life, he promises us that we will rule and reign in the next. But if we do not overcome, we will not be rewarded. Seeing that we have such a privilege and responsibility, let us rise and take hold of it. We need not fear, for God has guaranteed to help us in our high calling. Praise him for such encouragement!

STOP AND THINK

There is no greater privilege than sharing the feelings of God. Shall I grieve him by neglecting this, or please him by taking hold of it?

The Father Heart of God

by Floyd McClung

What is God like?

Has he got time for twentieth-century men and women?

Does he really care?

In his work with *Youth with a Mission*, Floyd McClung has met many who suffer from deep emotional hurts and fears.

Time and again it has been the discovery of God as Father—perfect and reliable, unlike any human parent—that has brought healing and liberty.

This book is for you...

...if you find it hard to accept God as a loving father, or
...if you know God's love but would like to share his blessing with others more effectively.

k

Kingsway Publications

God is my Father

by Nick Cuthbert

Today it is not only individuals who are insecure: whole nations tremble at the prospect of global war or international famine. The greatest minds are staggered by the immensity of mankind's problems. What hope, then, for those of us who simply want to lead peaceable and fulfilling lives?

Nick Cuthbert has proved God as a Father in his own life. Here he shows how that security can be yours too. Once we've joined the Father's family, we've placed ourselves into his care.

He will ... mend the broken places
     ... provide all we need
     ... speak to us clearly
     ... give us loving discipline.

Secure in God's family, we will be ready and able to reach out to the many others who do not yet enjoy a personal relationship with the living God.

Kingsway Publications